16089

DANTE GABRIEL ROSSETTI

Selected Poems and Translations

Edited with an Introduction by
Clive Wilmer

Fyfield Books

For Tony Tanner

First published in 1991 by
Carcanet Press Limited
208-212 Corn Exchange Buildings
Manchester M4 3BQ

British Library Cataloguing in Publication Data
Rossetti, D.G. *1828-1882*
    Selected poems and translations.
    I. Title   II. Wilmer, Clive
    828.91409

    ISBN 0 85635 915 7

The Publisher acknowledges financial assistance from
the Arts Council of Great Britain.

Typeset in 10pt Palatino by Bryan Williamson, Darwen
Printed and bound in England by SRP Ltd, Exeter

Contents

TRANSLATIONS

Introduction

For many of his contemporaries, Dante Gabriel Rossetti was a heroic figure. That is not, I suppose, how he is thought of today. Few of the great Victorians have fared well in the twentieth century, but Rossetti's stock has fallen more than most and, though in the past twenty years or so his pictures have to some extent recovered, his verse has not even been in print for most of that period.

But in the later nineteenth century, a succession of artistic groupings looked to Rossetti as their leader. The Pre-Raphaelite Brotherhood of 1848, founded by Rossetti with Holman Hunt and Millais, was the paradigm for subsequent rebellions. It was, in many ways, the first of the modern movements in the arts. For one thing, the Pre-Raphaelites defied the establishment of their day, presuming to follow aesthetic standards endorsed by neither academy nor market. For another, the art they aspired to emulate – that of medieval Italy – was generally thought of as primitive. They were also suspected of unorthodox political views: the realism with which they handled their Christian subjects smacked of socialism to some critics. The original Brotherhood turned out to be short-lived, but Rossetti's Pre-Raphaelite charisma was to affect artistic life in England for more than three generations – from Morris and Burne-Jones in the following decade, through Pater and the Aesthetes, to Yeats and the young Ezra Pound at the start of the present century. For all of them, Rossetti represented an ideal: that of solitary dedication to art and beauty, sometimes against the odds. He was no polemicist and lacked the public courage of Wilde or Ruskin. His strength lay in his indifference to reverence and success. The mere existence of his work implied a criticism of the age for its ugliness, philistine materialism and brutality. It is a strange irony that, without Rossetti, the Modernists who dethroned him would have lacked a great example.

Gabriel Charles Dante Rossetti was born in London in 1828. He was the second of four children, all of whom had literary aspirations.

It was an extraordinary family. The mother, born Frances Mary Lavinia Polidori, was half-Italian and bilingual, though her upbringing and education had been English. A devout Anglican with a strong feeling for literature, she brought her children up to be English like herself, in spite of the fact that they were three-quarters Italian. (Dante Gabriel never visited Italy, in spite of the obvious motives for doing so.) The father, Gabriele Rossetti, was an enthusiast for Italian liberty whose political activities in the Kingdom of Naples had forced him into exile. He was attracted to religions of a vaguely mystical nature and had progressed through free-thinking and Freemasonry to a pot-pourri of his own, oriental and Swedenborgian in tendency. It is worth remarking that while Dante Gabriel's taste for Catholic symbolism was clearly learnt from his mother, he was his father's son in the 'mild but muddled awe' – the phrase is from Evelyn Waugh's biography – with which he confronted the great issues of life. His sister Christina, whose poetry is rich with the spirit of her mother's Anglicanism, was in this respect better served.

Gabriele Rossetti was also an authority on Dante and wrote four books about him. He seems to have read the *Comedy* in quest of ciphers that – so he argued – disclosed the poet's 'secret' political and religious beliefs, which of course foreshadowed his own. The children grew up in an atmosphere steeped in Dante and political rumour, with their home a talking-shop for exiled Italian patriots. Dante Gabriel absorbed the poetry but, though he sympathized with his father's radicalism, made it a principle to preserve his art from all systematic belief.

Frances Rossetti had been brought up an Evangelical but was stirred in adulthood by the Oxford Movement. In this she resembled many of her contemporaries, who thus unconsciously combined Catholic forms with Protestant idealism. It is a combination to be found in her son's earliest paintings and in his verse apology for them, 'Old and New Art'. In 1846, very much in that frame of mind, he enrolled in the Antique School of the Royal Academy. Always impatient with external disciplines, he soon tired of drawing from antique casts. Before long he had left the school and was sitting at the feet of the 27-year-old Ford Madox Brown. Brown had the mixture of spiritual idealism and boisterous earthiness that always attracted Rossetti. His pictures, with their sharpness of outline and unshaded brilliance of colour, appealed to a young man bored with the dingy chiaroscuro of English academic classicism. Brown had been taught by the German Nazarenes in Rome to value medieval and early Renaissance painters, whose art was then looked upon as 'primitive'. The richly coloured world of such pictures, with their Catholic imagery, enchanted Rossetti and blended in his mind with the Romantic fashion for the Middle Ages, to which Anglo-Catholic ritual in part belonged. It is hardly surprising that he soon encountered other young painters subject to the same trends and, drawn like his father to conspiratorial atmospheres, founded with them (half in jest) a secret Brotherhood, whose aim was to subvert the Academy.

As it turned out, Rossetti had little in common with Holman Hunt and less with Millais, but the effects of their boyish rebellion were considerable. The Brotherhood had been formed in 1848, the year of revolutions. At the Academy exhibition of 1849, the unexplained initials P.R.B. on their paintings caused the critics to over-react absurdly. Their reviews attracted the attention of John Ruskin, already the most influential critic of the day, who, when he saw the paintings, recognized many of his own values in them. In two letters to the *Times* he sprang to their defence and, in effect, made their names for them.

Their brief moment of brotherly success ensured that a most peculiar hotch-potch of preoccupations would for later generations seem a coherent programme: naturalism in painting, the Italian 'primitives', Gothic architecture, Anglo-Catholic symbolism, ethical socialism, the Arthurian myth, Dante and Chaucer, anti-materialism, anti-industrialism, the social value of beauty, and so on. To all this Rossetti added two personal convictions. He believed – no doubt following Coleridge – that creativity is a fundamental part of human nature and that, given favourable circumstances, we can all acquire the necessary techniques to flesh out our visions. Secondly, he took it for granted that all art, literature and design have the same roots and belong in community with one another. Thus one of the earliest Pre-Raphaelite enterprises was the short-lived magazine

The Germ (1850), which published poetry, prose and drawings by the Brothers and their associates. The first issue included, *inter alia*, 'The Blessed Damozel' and Christina Rossetti's 'A Pause of Thought'. At the same time, Rossetti was writing poems as 'captions' for his own paintings and sonnets on other pictures he admired. This community of the arts was to be resumed with increased vitality in 1857 when he came into contact with two young disciples studying at Oxford, Edward Burne-Jones and William Morris. Through these new friendships, and particularly through the multi-talented energies of Morris, Pre-Raphaelite ideals were to outlast the century. It can be argued indeed that they have not been absent from our own; one thinks of the Vorticists and their journal *Blast*, the Ditchling community of Eric Gill and – on the debit side – the sickly nostalgia of the Ruralist Brotherhood.

It was in 1850 that Rossetti met Elizabeth Siddal, a beautiful young milliner's assistant. Possessed of magnificent reddish-blonde hair and a pale unearthly complexion, she soon became the archetypal Pre-Raphaelite model. Under Rossetti's influence, the relatively uneducated girl revealed a talent for poetry and drawing, thus demonstrating one of his most cherished theories. But the relationship was to prove unhappy. The streak of Latin sensuality in Rossetti's temperament accorded ill with the chivalrous idealism he and his friends proclaimed. The result was an excessively long and guilt-stricken engagement, aggravated by poverty, by Lizzy's ill-health and by Rossetti's repeated infidelities. He began to doubt his talent as a painter and experienced a conflict in his creative economy between painting and poetry. Ironically, it now seems his most fruitful period: the time of his first works in watercolour, the wonderfully intimate drawings of Lizzy Siddal, and his best lyrical poems – 'The Woodspurge', 'Sudden Light' and 'The Honeysuckle' – all of which reflect the vagaries of their relationship.

In 1860 Rossetti finally married her. He clearly did so out of a misguided sense of duty, for the famous beauty was already beginning to fade. The following year she gave birth to a still-born child. Then in 1862, already heavily dependent on laudanum, she took an overdose of the drug and died. The coroner's verdict was accidental death but Rossetti took it for suicide and blamed himself for it: because of his preoccupation with his poetry, because of other women, because of the inadequacy of his love. Many of the other women were 'rescued' prostitutes, a class of woman he was drawn to, but it seems almost certain that by 1862 he was in love with Jane Morris – with the wife, that is to say, of one of his closest friends. Out of these emotional complexities came the richest of his poetic achievements, the sonnet-sequence 'The House of Life'. Rossetti worked on this sequence for the whole of his creative life – from 1848 to 1881 – but the tension that gives it its dramatic substance comes from the presence alongside Lizzy Siddal of a second and secret love. This *Innominata* (as Paull Franklin Baum calls her) may represent a number of different women, but that she is mainly Jane Morris can no longer seriously be denied. Janey now became the main subject of his painting and, between 1871 and 1874, the period when William Morris was often travelling in Iceland, Rossetti shared the Morris family home of Kelmscott Manor.

The story of Rossetti's later life is a painful one. He had always had a morbid streak, but its effects had been outweighed by his good qualities: warmth, charm, unconventionality, a talent for conversation, a boyish and irreverent sense of fun and, beneath it all, an idealism without trace of pomposity. Now, tormented by guilt, he became subject to chronic insomnia. A few important friendships sustained him throughout his final years, but for much of the time he lived out a punishing solitude. The paintings of the period – the brooding icons of Janey as various goddesses and *femmes fatales* – are haunted and dense with despair, and the same is true of much of 'The House of Life'. The contrast with his early work, its freshness like a medieval tapestry's, could not be more disheartening. The poems return again and again to the problem of sleeplessness, which Rossetti sought to cure with increasingly large doses of chloral and whisky. But these only aggravated the problem. In 1871 a prurient attack on the 'fleshiness' of his poetry (a particular object was the sonnet 'Nuptial Sleep') had wounded him deeply, disturbing him no doubt with its grain of truth. This led to a suicide attempt and a nervous breakdown. Under these pressures his health began to fail, but it was not until 1882 that it finally gave way. He was only fifty-four when he died.

Rossetti's career as a poet really begins with his translations. *The Early Italian Poets* (later re-titled *Dante and his Circle*) appeared in 1861 when he was 33, but he seems to have embarked on the work as early as 1846. According to his brother William Michael, who edited his *Works*, the bulk of the poems were complete by 1848, though he seems to have carried on working at them till 1850. When the book eventually appeared, as William Michael tells us, 'it was recognized that the poetical faculty evinced in it was something more than that of a simple translator'. This success encouraged Rossetti to push on with his own poems. By the time of Lizzy's death he had assembled a substantial collection but – the macabre story is well-known – blaming his poetry for her suicide, he buried the book in her coffin. When in the mid 1860s, moved by his feelings for Janey Morris, he began writing sonnets again, his friends persuaded him to have the book exhumed and in 1870 he published his first collection, which he called simply *Poems*. In 1881 this was expanded to two volumes, *Poems* and *Ballads and Sonnets*, the latter containing new poems and the completed text of 'The House of Life'.

Rossetti's translation of the *Vita Nuova* (The New Life) was the first English translation of Dante's first great work. For most English readers until that time, Dante was the author of *The Divine Comedy* and nothing else. To 'The New Life' Rossetti added a selection of short lyrics by the young Dante and other poets of his circle, notably Guido Cavalcanti and Cino da Pistoia. These are the thirteenth century Tuscan poets praised in the *Purgatorio* for their 'sweet new style' (*dolce stil novo*). Rossetti then went on to translate some of their Sicilian and Central Italian precursors, all of them dialect poets but effectively the first to write in Italian vernacular. These earlier poets mostly deal with the same limited theme – the lover's devotion to his lady – but are brilliantly inventive in their formal schemes. In both these respects they are largely dependent on the Provençal Troubadours of the previous century. The thematic range was deepened and extended in the work of the Bolognese poet Guido Guinizelli (or Guinicelli), to whom Dante and Cavalcanti looked as their master. The values they share with him are summed up in his great 'Canzone: Of the Gentle Heart', one of Rossetti's *tours de force* as a translator. Our worth as human beings, for Guinizelli, has nothing to do with lineage or wealth but with the refinement of our natural disposition. Our capacity for love, in this view of the world, is an index of our spiritual nobility, our 'gentleness'. It is not difficult to see how, from these notions, the idea develops of the lover living a life of service to a lady who may never acknowledge it, let alone reward it; nor of how what began as a kind of attachment, adulterous in spirit if not in practice, was to become through Dante's Beatrice a model of divine love: one which, correctly understood, might lead the lover to his own salvation.

There can be no doubt that Rossetti in some respects dilutes the philosophical force of his originals. Some key terms are inherently untranslatable: *virtú*, for instance, which means spiritual potency, or *gentile*, which is noble or refined; Rossetti translates these 'virtue' and 'gentle', justified in that our modern usage has grown from these early poems and their influence, but lacking the concrete force of the Italian. His heavily Romantic archaising diction, moreover, misses the lightness and colloquial vigour of early Italian speech. But few translators can be said to have so memorably naturalized the vision and experience of a culture remote from our own. The best comparison is Pound's *Cathay*, and Rossetti is among the very few translators not shamed by that comparison. But, as William Michael said of them, 'the translations serve...as a kind of prologue to Rossetti's personality among the English poets.' In other words, Rossetti learnt his craft in the translator's *atelier*. A close examination of his work will reveal that almost all his important characteristics have their roots in his first serious literary endeavour.

These characteristics may be summarized under four headings: (1) formal invention; (2) the play of allegory with autobiography; (3) the sublimation of sexual love; (4) intense particularity of images.

The first of these is less important for Rossetti's own poetry than it is for the translations themselves and their influence on Modernist poets such as Pound and Bunting. Every one of

13

Rossetti's versions follows his original in rhyme-scheme, line-length and stanzaic pattern. Since the rhyme-schemes of early medieval poetry are often elaborate, with lace-like patterns of internal rhyme offsetting the rhymed endings, the translations represent a remarkable achievement of craftsmanship. One could argue, indeed, that the ultimate cost to Rossetti was too great, for his own poems sometimes suffer in rhythmic variety and *élan* from an over-precise attention to formal prescription. Nevertheless, the exercise of this discipline led to kinds of stanzaic movement which modern critics have thought of as absent from English verse between Traherne and Hopkins. Take these lines from Jacopo Lentino, a Sicilian of the mid-Thirteenth Century:

> For Love has made me weep
> With sighs that do him wrong,
> Since, when most strong my joy, he gave this woe.
> I am broken, as a ship
> Perishing of the song,
> Sweet, sweet and long the songs the sirens know.
> The mariner forgets,
> Voyaging in those straits,
> And dies assuredly.
> Yea, from her pride perverse,
> Who hath my heart as hers,
> Even such my death must be.

The movement in that first sentence, the forcing of syntax against stanza, represents a kind of internal drama that recalls Metaphysical poetry.

The second and third characteristics, autobiography and sublimated love, are both Dantesque and may be treated together. Instead of the vast Thomist summation of reality in which Dante's private passion takes its place, we have a sublimation of erotic feeling that is purely subjective. That the vision is vastly inferior cannot be denied, but it is sentimental to suppose (as Rossetti clearly did not) that the Dantesque unity could be attained in the modern world. Like his Modernist successors, Rossetti took from Dante those things that were available to him in his own experience and constructed his own subjective and fragmented universe out of them. Rossetti's is a poetry which admits that for us today there are no universal explanations.

> Cling heart to heart; nor of this hour demand
>> Whether in very truth, when we are dead,
>> Our hearts shall wake to know Love's golden head
> Sole sunshine of the imperishable land;
> Or but discern, through night's unfeatured scope,
> Scorn-fired at length the illusive eyes of Hope.

Much of what he learned from the Italians is there: not only the blend of image and abstraction, but the play of allegory and personification which he found in the *Vita Nuova*, where Love, 'a spiritual essence', is represented as 'a thing outward and visible'. Dante constructs an allegory out of the facts of his own life; Rossetti in 'The House of Life' does something analogous, but there is no 'lady round whom splendours move / In homage' at the end of it to foreshadow a great vision of the Love that moves the stars. Dante, within this context risks the charge of blasphemy (comparing an earthly woman to the Redeemer, as he does by implication in 'I felt a spirit of love begin to stir') but his devotional context permits a narrow escape. Guinizelli lets himself off less lightly with a prayer:

> Then may I plead: 'As though from thee he came,
>> Love wore an angel's face:
> Lord, if I loved her, count it not my shame.'

Rossetti in the fantasy heaven of 'The Blessed Damozel' would plainly stand accused, were it not for the fact that we never begin to take it seriously. The reason why there is no risk becomes clearer when we turn to 'The Portrait', where the immortality of the loved woman is secured by a work of art. As far as the immortality of the soul is concerned, Rossetti neither affirms nor denies it. So, where in Dante or Guinizelli sexual love and the beauty of the lady foreshadow the love of God and the kingdom of heaven, in Rossetti they prepare us for the religion of Art:

Here with her face doth memory sit
   Meanwhile, and wait the day's decline,
Till other eyes shall look from it,
   Eyes of the spirit's Palestine,
Even than the old gaze tenderer;
While hopes and aims long lost with her
   Stand round her image side by side,
   Like tombs of pilgrims that have died
About the Holy Sepulchre.

Aestheticism, though it expresses a religious sensibility, is as far removed from actual religion as it is possible to be. The conviction that the world has meaning, as it occurs in Dante or – to compare another Victorian – in Ruskin, brings with it a sense of the world's substantial otherness. Dante's symbolism is that of a realist, not a nominalist; he does not invent symbols but assumes that the things of this world already possess the meanings he deploys in his poem. Beatrice is not *like* an angel; in essence and potentiality she *is* an angel. For Ruskin, a painting by Turner is devotional because it represents an act of attention to what is other. It is truly 'a window on the world', so framed that the alert and sensitive spectator may 'read' the landscape and depart with a profounder knowledge of the whole of nature. By contrast, Rossetti's 'portrait' is a mirror. Displayed within its frame is the consciousness of the person who contemplates it. It denies objective reality and transforms the things of the world to fictive symbols, exponents of consciousness. It is no accident that mirrors and reflections figure prominently in Rossetti's work: 'Look in my face; my name is Might-have-been; / I am also called No-more, Too-late, Farewell...' ('A Superscription'). In this he anticipates one of his disciples. Walter Pater's famous account of the *Mona Lisa* describes that lady as if she were a Rossettian *femme fatale* whose presence merely reflects 'what in the ways of a thousand years men had come to desire'; and indeed, Rossetti writes in similar terms of his own picture *Lady Lilith* in 'Body's Beauty'.

The analogy with painting is important because Rossetti's imagination was clearly stimulated by the interaction of word and visual image. A poem like 'Silent Noon', for instance, almost persuades the reader to frame and compose the scene described. Pater, in a fine essay on Rossetti, draws attention to this quality in the earliest of his poems:

> One of the peculiarities of *The Blessed Damozel* was a definiteness of sensible imagery, which seemed almost grotesque to some, and was strange, above all, in a theme so profoundly visionary. The gold bar of heaven from which she leaned, her hair yellow like ripe corn, are but examples of a general treatment, as naïvely detailed as the pictures of those early painters contemporary with Dante, who has shown a similar care for minute and definite imagery in his verse; there, too, in the very midst of profoundly mystic vision... For Rossetti, as for Dante, without question on his part, the first condition of the poetic way of seeing and presenting things is particularisation.

This brings us to the fourth of Rossetti's 'early Italian' characteristics: particularization. And immediately we find a paradox: the sensuous visionary. If we take a look at some later poets, Hopkins, say, or Pound, we are unlikely to be impressed by Rossetti's particulars. It cannot be argued that he cleanses our perceptions as they do, for his images, sharp and fresh as they sometimes are, serve another purpose. In such poems as 'The Stream's Secret' and 'Love's Nocturn' (Pater goes on to say) Rossetti sets Love on to 'inquire what lies *below the surface* of sleep, and *below* the water; stream or dream being forced to speak by Love's powerful "control"...' (my italics). In the outcome, says Pater, 'One seems to hear... a really new kind of poetic utterance, with effects which have nothing else like them...' This new kind of utterance, it seems to me, is a foretaste of what in French poetry, taken much farther, came to be known as Symbolism. As in Symbolist verse, a loss of the world in dream and inwardness expresses itself through the particulars of sensuous experience.

When Pater compares this device of Rossetti's to Dante, we should think not so much of Dante himself but of Dante in Rossetti's translation: for instance, his brilliant version of the 'Sestina: Of the Lady Pietra degli Scrovigni':

> When on her hair she sets a crown of grass
> The thought has no more room for other lady,
> Because she weaves the yellow with the green
> So well that love sits down there in the shade, –
> Love who has shut me in among low hills
> Faster than between walls of granite-stone.

The image of garlanded hair is, to play with anachronism, strikingly Pre-Raphaelite and is surely the source, by way of Keats, of the poem Pater cites:

> Her robe, ungirt from clasp to hem,
>   No wrought flowers did adorn,
> But a white rose of Mary's gift,
>   For service meetly worn;
> Her hair that lay along her back
>   Was yellow like ripe corn.

The Pre-Raphaelites and their followers in the Arts and Crafts movement were much taken with an aspect of medieval culture that has been called Franciscan: the loving attention to natural detail as an index of the love of God. This is the feeling that validates, for instance, the lists of good things in the sonnets of Folgore da San Geminiano, at least as Rossetti translates them. In Rossetti's own poetry, though, it is the absence of God or meaning that renders the images so poignant, makes of them such accurate registers of mood and feeling. Again, the source is in the *stilnovisti*: the freshness of perception in the first few lines of that stanza from Dante's sestina lays the reader open to the claustrophobic closure in the last two. Rossetti turns this characteristic to his own ends, which resemble those of a Symbolist such as Mallarmé. The exquisitely detailed natural description becomes – to use a post-Symbolist phrase – an objective correlative for a state of mind. For example:

> Her thought, long stagnant, stirred by speech,
>   Gave her a sick recoil;
> As, dip thy fingers through the green
> That masks a pool, – where they have been
> The naked depth is black between.

The quotation is from 'The Bride's Prelude', an unfinished narrative poem. Like most of Rossetti's attempts at narrative, it is a failure, mainly because it is too long and so highly wrought that the narrative thrust gets clogged with detail. It was the detail that interested him, because that was how he represented states of mind; and to no state of mind did he return more often than to stagnation, especially when occasioned (as here) by sexual guilt. Thus the subject of the poem becomes, in effect, the cause of its failure as storytelling. Of all his narratives, only 'Jenny' and 'Sister Helen' approach success, and this is surely because in both cases the story is left to inference; Rossetti is allowed to concentrate on moments and states of mind in which the meaning of past events is clarified.

The other side of the coin can be found in another fragment, 'The Orchard Pit', an extraordinarily powerful parable of demonic sexuality. Rossetti wrote out the plot of the poem in prose but presumably found himself unable to get it all into verse. Yet, as a comparison of the prose with the poem reveals, he had said everything that needed saying. 'The Orchard Pit' is a lyric, not a narrative, and lyric poetry is what Rossetti was good at. He calls the sonnet 'a moment's monument', but the phrase applies to all his better poems.

In the first chapter of his *After Babel*, George Steiner cites a poem of Rossetti's as an example of how certain periods of our literature have become so remote for us that their writings need 'translation'.

> We are, in the main, 'word-blind' to Pre-Raphaelite and Decadent verse. This blindness results from a major change in habits of sensibility. Our contemporary sense of the poetic, our often unexamined presumptions about valid or spurious uses of figurative speech have developed from a conscious negation of *fin-de-siècle* ideals. It was precisely with the rejection, by the Modernist movement, of Victorian and post-Victorian aesthetics that the new astringency and insistence on verifiable structure came into force.

In an era that has seen Morris fabrics return to our armchairs and

Gustave Moreau in the same galleries as Monet and Degas, these observations, true as they may once have been, begin to seem strangely dated. Earlier in the chapter, Steiner says of the poem in question ('For *Ruggiero and Angelica*') that 'Nothing is being said in these fourteen lines; no expressive needs are being served'. But surely the opposite is the case: Rossetti has more to say than his overt subject is able to bear. What Steiner dislikes is the 'uncleansed' language, stiff with poeticism and archaic turns of phrase, that typifies Rossetti. Today we are beginning to see the point of such language, with its shocking clarities offset by its blurs; for, much of the time, Rossetti is struggling with obscurities of the psyche which our age has seen explored in other ways.

Where Modernism is concerned, moreover, Steiner's remarks are not strictly speaking true. The Modernists certainly reacted against Victorian diction, but it is also the case that poems such as 'For *Ruggiero and Angelica*' opened the way for the visionary subject matter of, for instance, W.B. Yeats in a poem such as 'The Second Coming'. Early Yeats is distinctly Pre-Raphaelite anyway, and for Pound the work done by Rossetti in making a certain sensibility, Latin and medieval, available to English and to modern writing was invaluable. When Pound quotes Guinizelli's great Canzone in Canto LI, he uses Rossetti's version, and it should not be forgotten that the medieval poets Pound advocated throughout his life first came to him through Rossetti – Cavalcanti, the young Dante, François Villon. Even Eliot confessed that Rossetti had been a key influence on the poems of his adolescence; it is tempting to speculate on the part Pre-Raphaelite poems may have played in Eliot's attempts to create an English equivalent for the language of the Symbolists.

The value of 'For *Ruggiero and Angelica*' is largely historical, but Rossetti also wrote major works of art – 'A Superscription', 'The Orchard Pit', 'The Portrait', 'Sudden Light', 'The Woodspurge'. In certain of these poems he achieves something of revolutionary import. As early as the bracketed stanzas of 'The Blessed Damozel' he had shown the mind making symbols of its accidental experiences. This led in time to whole poems of unexplained, often uncontextualized description – 'Near Brussels: A Half-way

Pause', 'Autumn Idleness', 'The Honeysuckle' – in which the accurate rendering of an external scene provides the index for a subjective emotion. Then, in 'The Woodspurge', he allows himself to reflect on his procedure. The poem deals with an incommunicable feeling of sorrow for which the woodspurge becomes the objective symbol. It is not archetypal, and it does not resemble the emotion in any way. It acquires its significance fortuitously, through subjective association. This is in a sense the beginning of post-Christian, post-classical poetry in English: the moment when it becomes possible to write a poem that does not move from experience to meaning but is on the contrary concerned with the absence of meaning, with the impossibility in some circumstances of making sense of what happens to us. Rossetti was not the first poet to do this – Browning, for example, had done it before him in 'Love in a Life' and 'Two in the Campagna'. But Rossetti's special status for the artists of his time gave his innovation an impact denied to Browning. We are just beginning to be able to feel that impact again.

CLIVE WILMER
Cambridge 1990

Note on the text

The text used for this edition is *The Works of Dante Gabriel Rossetti*, edited by William M. Rossetti (London, 1911). As his brother tells us in the Preface, Rossetti was a fastidious poet and revised his work constantly: so some alternative versions are to be found in anthologies and critical works. Indeed the last readily available edition, the Oxford University Press *Poems*, was based on the text of 1870, which is very different from those of 1881 and 1911.

I had hoped to organize my selection chronologically, but the long-drawn-out composition of *The House of Life* made this impossible. A similar problem affects the 'Sonnets on Pictures'. For the other poems I have usually followed chronology, but have felt free to diverge from it occasionally in the interests of generic comparison. The Italian poems follow the order of the first edition, *The Early Italian Poets* (1861), a reprint of which is currently published by Anvil Press Poetry, edited by Sally Purcell (London, 1981). The 'Ballata: Of his Lady among other Ladies' is no longer ascribed to Guido Cavalcanti.

Suggestions for further reading

Walter Pater, 'Dante Gabriel Rossetti', *Appreciations, with an Essay on Style* (London, 1889). Still the best critical essay.

Oswald Doughty, *A Victorian Romantic: Dante Gabriel Rossetti* (London, 1949). A critical biography.

Rosalie Glynn Grylls, *Portrait of Rossetti* (London, 1964). A good popular biography.

Joan Rees, *The Poetry of Dante Gabriel Rossetti: Modes of Self-expression* (Cambridge, 1981). A critical study.

Tim Hilton, *The Pre-Raphaelites* (London, 1970). A brief, well-illustrated study of the schools of painting.

Alicia Craig Faxon, *Dante Gabriel Rossetti* (Oxford, 1989). A monograph on the paintings, opulently illustrated.

from
The House of Life:
A SONNET SEQUENCE

A Sonnet is a moment's monument, –
  Memorial from the Soul's eternity
  To one dead deathless hour. Look that it be,
Whether for lustral rite or dire portent,
Of its own arduous fulness reverent:
  Carve it in ivory or in ebony,
  As Day or Night may rule; and let Time see
Its flowering crest impearled and orient.

A Sonnet is a coin: its face reveals
  The soul, – its converse, to what Power 'tis due: –
Whether for tribute to the august appeals
  Of Life, or dower in Love's high retinue,
It serve; or, 'mid the dark wharf's cavernous breath,
In Charon's palm it pay the toll to Death.

PART I
Youth and Change

I   *Love Enthroned*

I marked all kindred Powers the heart finds fair: –
  Truth, with awed lips; and Hope, with eyes upcast;
  And Fame, whose loud wings fan the ashen Past
To signal-fires, Oblivion's flight to scare;
And Youth, with still some single golden hair
  Unto his shoulder clinging, since the last
  Embrace wherein two sweet arms held him fast;
And Life, still wreathing flowers for Death to wear.

Love's throne was not with these; but far above
   All passionate wind of welcome and farewell
He sat in breathless bowers they dream not of;
    Though Truth foreknow Love's heart, and Hope foretell,
    And Fame be for Love's sake desirable,
And Youth be dear, and Life be sweet to Love.

VI   *The Kiss*

What smouldering senses in death's sick delay
   Or seizure of malign vicissitude
   Can rob this body of honour, or denude
This soul of wedding-raiment worn to-day?
For lo! even now my lady's lips did play
   With these my lips such consonant interlude
   As laurelled Orpheus longed for when he wooed
The half-drawn hungering face with that last lay.

I was a child beneath her touch, – a man
   When breast to breast we clung, even I and she, –
   A spirit when her spirit looked through me, –
A god when all our life-breath met to fan
Our life-blood, till love's emulous ardours ran,
   Fire within fire, desire in deity.

VIa   *Nuptial Sleep*

At length their long kiss severed, with sweet smart:
   And as the last slow sudden drops are shed
   From sparkling eaves when all the storm has fled,
So singly flagged the pulses of each heart.
Their bosoms sundered, with the opening start
   Of married flowers to either side outspread
   From the knit stem; yet still their mouths, burnt red,
Fawned on each other where they lay apart.

Sleep sank them lower than the tide of dreams,
   And their dreams watched them sink, and slid away.
Slowly their souls swam up again, through gleams
   Of watered light and dull drowned waifs of day;
Till from some wonder of new woods and streams
   He woke, and wondered more: for there she lay.

X   *The Portrait*

O Lord of all compassionate control,
   O Love! let this my lady's picture glow
   Under my hand to praise her name, and show
Even of her inner self the perfect whole:
That he who seeks her beauty's furthest goal,
   Beyond the light that the sweet glances throw
   And refluent wave of the sweet smile, may know
The very sky and sea-line of her soul.

Lo! it is done. Above the enthroning throat
   The mouth's mould testifies of voice and kiss,
   The shadowed eyes remember and foresee.
Her face is made her shrine. Let all men note
   That in all years (O Love, thy gift is this!)
   They that would look on her must come to me.

XIV   *Youth's Spring-Tribute*

On this sweet bank your head thrice sweet and dear
   I lay, and spread your hair on either side,
   And see the newborn woodflowers bashful-eyed
Look through the golden tresses here and there.
On these debateable borders of the year
   Spring's foot half falters; scarce she yet may know
   The leafless blackthorn-blossom from the snow;
And through her bowers the wind's way still is clear.

But April's sun strikes down the glades to-day;
    So shut your eyes upturned, and feel my kiss
Creep, as the Spring now thrills through every spray,
    Up your warm throat to your warm lips: for this
    Is even the hour of Love's sworn suitservice,
With whom cold hearts are counted castaway.

XIX *Silent Noon*

Your hands lie open in the long fresh grass, –
    The finger-points look through like rosy blooms:
    Your eyes smile peace. The pasture gleams and glooms
'Neath billowing skies that scatter and amass.
All round our nest, far as the eye can pass,
    Are golden kingcup-fields with silver edge
    Where the cow-parsley skirts the hawthorn-hedge.
'Tis visible silence, still as the hour-glass.

Deep in the sun-searched growths the dragon-fly
Hangs like a blue thread loosened from the sky: –
    So this wing'd hour is dropt to us from above.
Oh! clasp we to our hearts, for deathless dower,
This close-companioned inarticulate hour
    When twofold silence was the song of love.

XXV *Winged Hours*

Each hour until we meet is as a bird
    That wings from far his gradual way along
    The rustling covert of my soul, – his song
Still loudlier trilled through leaves more deeply stirr'd:
But at the hour of meeting, a clear word
    Is every note he sings, in Love's own tongue;
    Yet, Love, thou know'st the sweet strain suffers wrong,
Full oft through our contending joys unheard.

What of that hour at last, when for her sake
  No wing may fly to me nor song may flow;
  When, wandering round my life unleaved, I know
The bloodied feathers scattered in the brake,
And think how she, far from me, with like eyes
Sees through the untuneful bough the wingless skies?

XXVII   *Heart's Compass*

Sometimes thou seem'st not as thyself alone,
  But as the meaning of all things that are;
  A breathless wonder, shadowing forth afar
Some heavenly solstice hushed and halcyon;
Whose unstirred lips are music's visible tone;
  Whose eyes the sun-gate of the soul unbar,
  Being of its furthest fires oracular; –
The evident heart of all life sown and mown.

Even such Love is; and is not thy name Love?
  Yea, by thy hand the Love-god rends apart
  All gathering clouds of Night's ambiguous art;
Flings them far down, and sets thine eyes above;
And simply, as some gage of flower or glove,
  Stakes with a smile the world against thy heart.

XXXIV   *The Dark Glass*

Not I myself know all my love for thee:
  How should I reach so far, who cannot weigh
  To-morrow's dower by gage of yesterday?
Shall birth and death, and all dark names that be
As doors and windows bared to some loud sea,
  Lash deaf mine ears and blind my face with spray;
  And shall my sense pierce love, – the last relay
And ultimate outpost of eternity?

Lo! what am I to Love, the lord of all?
   One murmuring shell he gathers from the sand, –
   One little heart-flame sheltered in his hand.
Yet through thine eyes he grants me clearest call
And veriest touch of powers primordial
   That any hour-girt life may understand.

XXXVI   *Life-in-Love*

Not in thy body is thy life at all,
   But in this lady's lips and hands and eyes;
   Through these she yields thee life that vivifies
What else were sorrow's servant and death's thrall.
Look on thyself without her, and recall
   The waste remembrance and forlorn surmise
   That lived but in a dead-drawn breath of sighs
O'er vanished hours and hours eventual.

Even so much life hath the poor tress of hair
   Which, stored apart, is all love hath to show
   For heart-beats and for fire-heats long ago;
Even so much life endures unknown, even where,
'Mid change the changeless night environeth,
Lies all that golden hair undimmed in death.

XLIV   *Cloud and Wind*

Love, should I fear death most for you or me?
   Yet if you die, can I not follow you,
   Forcing the straits of change? Alas! but who
Shall wrest a bond from night's inveteracy,
Ere yet my hazardous soul put forth, to be
   Her warrant against all her haste might rue? –
   Ah! in your eyes so reached what dumb adieu,
What unsunned gyres of waste eternity?

And if I die the first, shall death be then
    A lampless watchtower whence I see you weep? –
    Or (woe is me!) a bed wherein my sleep
Ne'er notes (as death's dear cup at last you drain)
The hour when you too learn that all is vain
    And that Hope sows what Love shall never reap?

XLVII   *Broken Music*

The mother will not turn, who thinks she hears
    Her nursling's speech first grow articulate;
    But breathless with averted eyes elate
She sits, with open lips and open ears,
That it may call her twice. 'Mid doubts and fears
    Thus oft my soul has hearkened; till the song,
    A central moan for days, at length found tongue,
And the sweet music welled and the sweet tears.

But now, whatever while the soul is fain
    To list that wonted murmur, as it were
The speech-bound sea-shell's low importunate strain, –
    No breath of song, thy voice alone is there,
O bitterly beloved! and all her gain
    Is but the pang of unpermitted prayer.

XLVIII   *Death-in-Love*

There came an image in Life's retinue
    That had Love's wings and bore his gonfalon:
    Fair was the web, and nobly wrought thereon,
O soul-sequestered face, thy form and hue!
Bewildering sounds, such as Spring wakens to,
    Shook in its folds; and through my heart its power
    Sped trackless as the immemorable hour
When birth's dark portal groaned and all was new.

But a veiled woman followed, and she caught
   The banner round its staff, to furl and cling, –
   Then plucked a feather from the bearer's wing,
And held it to his lips that stirred it not,
And said to me, "Behold, there is no breath:
I and this Love are one, and I am Death."

XLIX, L, LI, LII   *Willowwood*

1

I sat with Love upon a woodside well,
   Leaning across the water, I and he;
   Nor ever did he speak nor looked at me,
But touched his lute wherein was audible
The certain secret thing he had to tell:
   Only our mirrored eyes met silently
   In the low wave; and that sound came to be
The passionate voice I knew; and my tears fell.

And at their fall, his eyes beneath grew hers;
And with his foot and with his wing-feathers
   He swept the spring that watered my heart's drouth.
Then the dark ripples spread to waving hair,
And as I stooped, her own lips rising there
   Bubbled with brimming kisses at my mouth.

2

And now Love sang: but his was such a song
   So meshed with half-remembrance hard to free,
   As souls disused in death's sterility
May sing when the new birthday tarries long.
And I was made aware of a dumb throng
   That stood aloof, one form by every tree,
   All mournful forms, for each was I or she,
The shades of those our days that had no tongue.

They looked on us, and knew us and were known;
    While fast together, alive from the abyss,
    Clung the soul-wrung implacable close kiss;
And pity of self through all made broken moan
Which said, "For once, for once, for once alone!"
    And still Love sang, and what he sang was this: –

3

"O ye, all ye that walk in Willowwood,
    That walk with hollow faces burning white;
What fathom-depth of soul-struck widowhood,
    What long, what longer hours, one lifelong night,
Ere ye again, who so in vain have wooed
    Your last hope lost, who so in vain invite
Your lips to that their unforgotten food,
    Ere ye, ere ye again shall see the light!

Alas! the bitter banks in Willowwood,
    With tear-spurge wan, with blood-wort burning red:
Alas! if ever such a pillow could
    Steep deep the soul in sleep till she were dead, –
Better all life forget her than this thing,
That Willowwood should hold her wandering!"

4

So sang he: and as meeting rose and rose
    Together cling through the wind's wellaway
    Nor change at once, yet near the end of day
The leaves drop loosened where the heart-stain glows, –
So when the song died did the kiss unclose;
    And her face fell back drowned, and was as grey
    As its grey eyes; and if it ever may
Meet mine again I know not if Love knows.

31

Only I know that I leaned low and drank
A long draught from the water where she sank,
   Her breath and all her tears and all her soul:
And as I leaned, I know I felt Love's face
Pressed on my neck with moan of pity and grace,
   Till both our heads were in his aureole.

LIII · *Without Her*

What of her glass without her? The blank grey
   There where the pool is blind of the moon's face.
   Her dress without her? The tossed empty space
Of cloud-rack whence the moon has passed away.
Her paths without her? Day's appointed sway
   Usurped by desolate night. Her pillowed place
   Without her? Tears, ah me! for love's good grace,
And cold forgetfulness of night or day.

What of the heart without her? Nay, poor heart,
   Of thee what word remains ere speech be still?
   A wayfarer by barren ways and chill,
Steep ways and weary, without her thou art,
Where the long cloud, the long wood's counterpart,
   Sheds doubled darkness up the labouring hill.

LIX *Love's Last Gift*

Love to his singer held a glistening leaf,
   And said: "The rose-tree and the apple-tree
   Have fruits to vaunt or flowers to lure the bee;
And golden shafts are in the feathered sheaf
Of the great harvest-marshal, the year's chief,
   Victorious Summer; aye, and 'neath warm sea
   Strange secret grasses lurk inviolably
Between the filtering channels of sunk reef.

All are my blooms; and all sweet blooms of love
   To thee I gave while Spring and Summer sang;
   But Autumn stops to listen, with some pang
From those worse things the wind is moaning of.
Only this laurel dreads no winter days:
Take my last gift; thy heart hath sung my praise."

PART II
Change and Fate

LX   *Transfigured Life*

As growth of form or momentary glance
   In a child's features will recall to mind
   The father's with the mother's face combin'd, –
Sweet interchange that memories still enhance:
And yet, as childhood's years and youth's advance,
   The gradual mouldings leave one stamp behind,
   Till in the blended likeness now we find
A separate man's or woman's countenance: –

So in the Song, the singer's Joy and Pain,
   Its very parents, evermore expand
To bid the passion's fullgrown birth remain,
   By Art's transfiguring essence subtly spann'd;
   And from that song-cloud shaped as a man's hand
There comes the sound as of abundant rain.

LXVII *The Landmark*

Was *that* the landmark? What, – the foolish well
   Whose wave, low down, I did not stoop to drink
   But sat and flung the pebbles from its brink
In sport to send its imaged skies pell-mell,
(And mine own image, had I noted well!) –
   Was that my point of turning? – I had thought
   The stations of my course should rise unsought,
As altar-stone or ensigned citadel.

But lo! the path is missed, I must go back,
   And thirst to drink when next I reach the spring
Which once I stained, which since may have grown black.
   Yet though no light be left nor bird now sing
   As here I turn, I'll thank God, hastening,
That the same goal is still on the same track.

LXIX *Autumn Idleness*

This sunlight shames November where he grieves
   In dead red leaves, and will not let him shun
   The day, though bough with bough be over-run.
But with a blessing every glade receives
High salutation; while from hillock-eaves
   The deer gaze calling, dappled white and dun,
   As if, being foresters of old, the sun
Had marked them with the shade of forest-leaves.

Here dawn to-day unveiled her magic glass;
   Here noon now gives the thirst and takes the dew;
Till eve bring rest when other good things pass.
   And here the lost hours the lost hours renew
While I still lead my shadow o'er the grass,
   Nor know, for longing, that which I should do.

LXX *The Hill Summit*

This feast-day of the sun, his altar there
   In the broad west has blazed for vesper-song;
   And I have loitered in the vale too long
And gaze now a belated worshipper.
Yet may I not forget that I was 'ware,
   So journeying, of his face at intervals
   Transfigured where the fringed horizon falls, –
A fiery bush with coruscating hair.

And now that I have climbed and won this height,
   I must tread downward through the sloping shade
And travel the bewildered tracks till night.
   Yet for this hour I still may here be stayed
   And see the gold air and the silver fade
And the last bird fly into the last light.

LXXIV, LXXV, LXXVI *Old and New Art*

1 ST LUKE THE PAINTER

Give honour unto Luke Evangelist;
   For he it was (the aged legends say)
   Who first taught Art to fold her hands and pray.
Scarcely at once she dared to rend the mist
Of devious symbols: but soon having wist
   How sky-breadth and field-silence and this day
   Are symbols also in some deeper way,
She looked through these to God and was God's priest.

And if, past noon, her toil began to irk,
   And she sought talismans, and turned in vain
      To soulless self-reflections of man's skill, –
      Yet now, in this the twilight, she might still
   Kneel in the latter grass to pray again,
Ere the night cometh and she may not work.

2 NOT AS THESE

"I am not as these are," the poet saith
  In youth's pride, and the painter, among men
  At bay, where never pencil comes nor pen,
And shut about with his own frozen breath.
To others, for whom only rhyme wins faith
  As poets, – only paint as painters, – then
  He turns in the cold silence; and again
Shrinking, "I am not as these are," he saith.

And say that this is so, what follows it?
  For were thine eyes set backwards in thine head,
    Such words were well; but they see on, and far.
Unto the lights of the great Past, new-lit
  Fair for the Future's track, look thou instead, –
    Say thou instead, "I am not as *these* are."

3 THE HUSBANDMEN

Though God, as one that is an householder,
  Called these to labour in His vineyard first,
  Before the husk of darkness was well burst
Bidding them grope their way out and bestir,
(Who, questioned of their wages, answered, "Sir,
  Unto each man a penny":) though the worst
  Burthen of heat was theirs and the dry thirst:
Though God has since found none such as these were
To do their work like them: – Because of this
  Stand not ye idle in the market-place.
    Which of ye knoweth *he* is not that last
Who may be first by faith and will? – yea, his
  The hand which after the appointed days
    And hours shall give a Future to their Past?

LXXVII   Soul's Beauty

Under the arch of Life, where love and death,
   Terror and mystery, guard her shrine, I saw
   Beauty enthroned; and though her gaze struck awe,
I drew it in as simply as my breath.
Hers are the eyes which, over and beneath,
   The sky and sea bend on thee, – which can draw,
   By sea or sky or woman, to one law,
The allotted bondman of her palm and wreath.

This is that Lady Beauty, in whose praise
   Thy voice and hand shake still, – long known to thee
     By flying hair and fluttering hem, – the beat
     Following her daily of thy heart and feet,
   How passionately and irretrievably,
In what fond flight, how many ways and days!

Written for Rossetti's picture, *Sibylla Palmifera*. [Ed.]

LXXVIII   Body's Beauty

Of Adam's first wife, Lilith, it is told
   (The witch he loved before the gift of Eve,)
   That, ere the snake's, her sweet tongue could deceive,
And her enchanted hair was the first gold.
And still she sits, young while the earth is old,
   And, subtly of herself contemplative,
   Draws men to watch the bright web she can weave,
Till heart and body and life are in its hold.

The rose and poppy are her flowers; for where
   Is he not found, O Lilith, whom shed scent
And soft-shed kisses and soft sleep shall snare?
   Lo! as that youth's eyes burned at thine, so went
   Thy spell through him, and left his straight neck bent
And round his heart one strangling golden hair.

Written for Rossetti's picture, *Lady Lilith*. [Ed.]

LXXIX *The Monochord*

Is it this sky's vast vault or ocean's sound
    That is Life's self and draws my life from me,
    And by instinct ineffable decree
Holds my breath quailing on the bitter bound?
Nay, is it Life or Death, thus thunder-crown'd,
    That 'mid the tide of all emergency
    Now notes my separate wave, and to what sea
Its difficult eddies labour in the ground?

Oh! what is this that knows the road I came,
The flame turned cloud, the cloud returned to flame,
    The lifted shifted steeps and all the way? –
That draws round me at last this wind-warm space,
And in regenerate rapture turns my face
    Upon the devious coverts of dismay?

LXXXI *Memorial Thresholds*

What place so strange, – though unrevealèd snow
    With unimaginable fires arise
    At the earth's end, – what passion of surprise
Like frost-bound fire-girt scenes of long ago?
Lo! this is none but I this hour; and lo!
    This is the very place which to mine eyes
    Those mortal hours in vain immortalize,
'Mid hurrying crowds, with what alone I know.

City, of thine a single simple door,
    By some new Power reduplicate, must be
    Even yet my life-porch in eternity,
Even with one presence filled, as once of yore:
Or mocking winds whirl round a chaff-strown floor
    Thee and thy years and these my words and me.

38

LXXXV *Vain Virtues*

What is the sorriest thing that enters Hell?
   None of the sins, – but this and that fair deed
   Which a soul's sin at length could supersede.
These yet are virgins, whom death's timely knell
Might once have sainted; whom the fiends compel
   Together now, in snake-bound shuddering sheaves
   Of anguish, while the pit's pollution leaves
Their refuse maidenhood abominable.

Night sucks them down, the tribute of the pit,
   Whose names, half entered in the book of Life,
     Were God's desire at noon. And as their hair
And eyes sink last, the Torturer deigns no whit
   To gaze, but, yearning, waits his destined wife,
     The Sin still blithe on earth that sent them there.

LXXXVI *Lost Days*

The lost days of my life until today,
   What were they, could I see them on the street
   Lie as they fell? Would they be ears of wheat
Sown once for food but trodden into clay?
Or golden coins squandered and still to pay?
   Or drops of blood dabbling the guilty feet?
   Or such spilt water as in dreams must cheat
The undying throats of Hell, athirst alway?

I do not see them here; but after death
   God knows I know the faces I shall see,
Each one a murdered self, with low last breath.
   "I am thyself, – what hast thou done to me?"
"And I – and I – thyself," (lo! each one saith,)
   "And thou thyself to all eternity!"

LXXXVII *Death's Songsters*

When first that horse, within whose populous womb
   The birth was death, o'ershadowed Troy with fate,
   Her elders, dubious of its Grecian freight,
Brought Helen there to sing the songs of home;
She whispered, "Friends, I am alone; come, come!"
   Then, crouched within, Ulysses waxed afraid,
   And on his comrades' quivering mouths he laid
His hands, and held them till the voice was dumb.

The same was he who, lashed to his own mast,
   There where the sea-flowers screen the charnel-caves,
Beside the sirens' singing island pass'd,
   Till sweetness failed along the inveterate waves....
Say, soul, – are songs of Death no heaven to thee,
Nor shames her lip the cheek of Victory?

XCI *Lost on Both Sides*

As when two men have loved a woman well,
   Each hating each, through Love's and Death's deceit;
   Since not for either this stark marriage-sheet
And the long pauses of this wedding-bell;
   Yet o'er her grave the night and day dispel
   At last their feud forlorn, with cold and heat;
   Nor other than dear friends to death may fleet
The two lives left that most of her can tell: –

So separate hopes, which in a soul had wooed
   The one same Peace, strove with each other long,
   And Peace before their faces perished since:
So through that soul, in restless brotherhood,
   They roam together now, and wind among
   Its bye-streets, knocking at the dusty inns.

XCV   *The Vase of Life*

Around the vase of Life at your slow pace
　He has not crept, but turned it with his hands,
　And all its sides already understands.
There, girt, one breathes alert for some great race;
Whose road runs far by sands and fruitful space;
　Who laughs, yet through the jolly throng has pass'd;
　Who weeps, nor stays for weeping; who at last,
A youth, stands somewhere crowned, with silent face.

And he has filled this vase with wine for blood,
　With blood for tears, with spice for burning vow,
　　With watered flowers for buried love most fit;
And would have cast it shattered to the flood,
　　Yet in Fate's name has kept it whole; which now
　　Stands empty till his ashes fall in it.

XCVII   *A Superscription*

Look in my face; my name is Might-have-been;
　I am also called No-more, Too-late, Farewell;
　Unto thine ear I hold the dead-sea shell
Cast up thy Life's foam-fretted feet between;
Unto thine eyes the glass where that is seen
　Which had Life's form and Love's, but by my spell
　Is now a shaken shadow intolerable,
Of ultimate things unuttered the frail screen.

Mark me, how still I am! But should there dart
　One moment through thy soul the soft surprise
　Of that winged Peace which lulls the breath of sighs, –
Then shalt thou see me smile, and turn apart
Thy visage to mine ambush at thy heart
　Sleepless with cold commemorative eyes.

Whence came his feet into my field, and why?
　　How is it that he sees it all so drear?
　　How do I see his seeing, and how hear
The name his bitter silence knows it by?
This was the little fold of separate sky
　　Whose pasturing clouds in the soul's atmosphere
　　Drew living light from one continual year:
How should he find it lifeless? He, or I?

Lo! this new Self now wanders round my field,
　　With plaints for every flower, and for each tree
　　A moan, the sighing wind's auxiliary:
And o'er sweet waters of my life, that yield
Unto his lips no draught but tears unseal'd,
　　Even in my place he weeps. Even I, not he.

The Blessed Damozel

The blessed damozel leaned out
   From the gold bar of Heaven;
Her eyes were deeper than the depth
   Of waters stilled at even;
She had three lilies in her hand,
   And the stars in her hair were seven.

Her robe, ungirt from clasp to hem,
   No wrought flowers did adorn,
But a white rose of Mary's gift,
   For service meetly worn;
Her hair that lay along her back
   Was yellow like ripe corn.

Herseemed she scarce had been a day
   One of God's choristers;
The wonder was not yet quite gone
   From that still look of hers;
Albeit, to them she left, her day
   Had counted as ten years.

(To one, it is ten years of years.
   ... Yet now, and in this place,
Surely she leaned o'er me – her hair
   Fell all about my face....
Nothing: the autumn-fall of leaves.
   The whole year sets apace.)

It was the rampart of God's house
   That she was standing on;
By God built over the sheer depth
   The which is Space begun;
So high, that looking downward thence
   She scarce could see the sun.

It lies in Heaven, across the flood
   Of ether, as a bridge.
Beneath, the tides of day and night
   With flame and darkness ridge
The void, as low as where this earth
   Spins like a fretful midge.

Around her, lovers, newly met
   'Mid deathless love's acclaims,
Spoke evermore among themselves
   Their heart-remembered names;
And the souls mounting up to God
   Went by her like thin flames.

And still she bowed herself and stooped
   Out of the circling charm;
Until her bosom must have made
   The bar she leaned on warm,
And the lilies lay as if asleep
   Along her bended arm.

From the fixed place of Heaven she saw
   Time like a pulse shake fierce
Through all the worlds. Her gaze still strove
   Within the gulf to pierce
Its path; and now she spoke as when
   The stars sang in their spheres.

The sun was gone now; the curled moon
   Was like a little feather
Fluttering far down the gulf; and now
   She spoke through the still weather.
Her voice was like the voice the stars
   Had when they sang together.

(Ah sweet! Even now, in that bird's song,
   Strove not her accents there,
Fain to be hearkened? When those bells

Possessed the mid-day air,
Strove not her steps to reach my side
   Down all the echoing stair?)

"I wish that he were come to me,
   For he will come," she said.
"Have I not prayed in Heaven? – on earth,
   Lord, Lord, has he not pray'd?
Are not two prayers a perfect strength?
   And shall I feel afraid?

"When round his head the aureole clings,
   And he is clothed in white,
I'll take his hand and go with him
   To the deep wells of light;
As unto a stream we will step down,
   And bathe there in God's sight.

"We two will stand beside that shrine,
   Occult, withheld, untrod,
Whose lamps are stirred continually
   With prayer sent up to God;
And see our old prayers, granted, melt
   Each like a little cloud.

"We two will lie i' the shadow of
   That living mystic tree
Within whose secret growth the Dove
   Is sometimes felt to be,
While every leaf that His plumes touch
   Saith His Name audibly.

"And I myself will teach to him,
   I myself, lying so,
The songs I sing here; which his voice
   Shall pause in, hushed and slow,
And find some knowledge at each pause,
   Or some new thing to know."

(Alas! we two, we two, thou say'st!
   Yea, one wast thou with me
That once of old. But shall God lift
   To endless unity
The soul whose likeness with thy soul
   Was but its love for thee?)

"We two," she said, "will seek the groves
   Where the lady Mary is,
With her five handmaidens, whose names
   Are five sweet symphonies,
Cecily, Gertrude, Magdalen,
   Margaret and Rosalys.

"Circlewise sit they, with bound locks
   And foreheads garlanded;
Into the fine cloth white like flame
   Weaving the golden thread,
To fashion the birth-robes for them
   Who are just born, being dead.

"He shall fear, haply, and be dumb
   Then will I lay my cheek
To his, and tell about our love,
   Not once abashed or weak:
And the dear Mother will approve
   My pride, and let me speak.

"Herself shall bring us, hand in hand,
   To Him round whom all souls
Kneel, the clear-ranged unnumbered heads
   Bowed with their aureoles:
And angels meeting us shall sing
   To their citherns and citoles.

"There will I ask of Christ the Lord
   Thus much for him and me: –
Only to live as once on earth

46

With Love, – only to be,
As then awhile, for ever now
   Together, I and he."

She gazed and listened and then said,
   Less sad of speech than mild, –
"All this is when he comes." She ceased.
   The light thrilled towards her, fill'd
With angels in strong level flight.
   Her eyes prayed, and she smil'd.

(I saw her smile.) But soon their path
   Was vague in distant spheres:
And then she cast her arms along
   The golden barriers,
And laid her face between her hands,
   And wept. (I heard her tears.)

My Sister's Sleep

She fell asleep on Christmas Eve.
   At length the long-ungranted shade
   Of weary eyelids overweigh'd
The pain nought else might yet relieve.

Our mother, who had leaned all day
   Over the bed from chime to chime,
   Then raised herself for the first time,
And as she sat her down, did pray.

Her little work-table was spread
   With work to finish. For the glare
   Made by her candle, she had care
To work some distance from the bed.

47

Without, there was a cold moon up,
   Of winter radiance sheer and thin;
   The hollow halo it was in
Was like an icy crystal cup.

Through the small room, with subtle sound
   Of flame, by vents the fireshine drove
   And reddened. In its dim alcove
The mirror shed a clearness round.

I had been sitting up some nights,
   And my tired mind felt weak and blank;
   Like a sharp strengthening wine it drank
The stillness and the broken lights.

Twelve struck. That sound, by dwindling years
   Heard in each hour, crept off; and then
   The ruffled silence spread again,
Like water that a pebble stirs.

Our mother rose from where she sat:
   Her needles, as she laid them down,
   Met lightly, and her silken gown
Settled: no other noise than that.

"Glory unto the Newly Born!"
   So, as said angels, she did say;
   Because we were in Christmas Day,
Though it would still be long till morn.

Just then in the room over us
   There was a pushing back of chairs,
   As some who had sat unawares
So late, now heard the hour, and rose.

With anxious softly-stepping haste
   Our mother went where Margaret lay,

Fearing the sounds o'erhead – should they
Have broken her long watched-for rest!

She stopped an instant, calm, and turned;
    But suddenly turned back again;
    And all her features seemed in pain
With woe, and her eyes gazed and yearned.

For my part, I but hid my face,
    And held my breath, and spoke no word:
    There was none spoken; but I heard
The silence for a little space.

Our mother bowed herself and wept:
    And both my arms fell, and I said,
    "God knows I knew that she was dead."
And there, all white, my sister slept.

Then kneeling, upon Christmas morn
    A little after twelve o'clock,
    We said, ere the first quarter struck,
"Christ's blessing on the newly born!"

Ave

Mother of the Fair Delight,
Thou handmaid perfect in God's sight,
Now sitting fourth beside the Three,
Thyself a woman-Trinity, –
Being a daughter born to God,
Mother of Christ from stall to rood,
And wife unto the Holy Ghost: –
Oh when our need is uttermost,
Think that to such as death may strike

Thou once wert sister sisterlike!
Thou headstone of humanity,
Groundstone of the great Mystery,
Fashioned like us, yet more than we!

Mind'st thou not (when June's heavy breath
Warmed the long days in Nazareth,)
That eve thou didst go forth to give
Thy flowers some drink that they might live
One faint night more amid the sands?
Far off the trees were as pale wands
Against the fervid sky: the sea
Sighed further off eternally
As human sorrow sighs in sleep.
Then suddenly the awe grew deep,
As of a day to which all days
Were footsteps in God's secret ways:
Until a folding sense, like prayer,
Which is, as God is, everywhere,
Gathered about thee; and a voice
Spake to thee without any noise,
Being of the silence: – "Hail," it said,
"Thou that art highly favourèd;
The Lord is with thee here and now;
Blessed among all women thou."

Ah! knew'st thou of the end, when first
That Babe was on thy bosom nurs'd? –
Or when He tottered round thy knee
Did thy great sorrow dawn on thee? –
And through His boyhood, year by year
Eating with Him the Passover,
Didst thou discern confusedly
That holier sacrament, when He,
The bitter cup about to quaff,
Should break the bread and eat thereof? –
Or came not yet the knowledge, even
Till on some day forecast in Heaven

His feet passed through thy door to press
Upon His Father's business? –
Or still was God's high secret kept?

Nay, but I think the whisper crept
Like growth through childhood. Work and play,
Things common to the course of day,
Awed thee with meanings unfulfill'd;
And all through girlhood, something still'd
Thy senses like the birth of light,
When thou hast trimmed thy lamp at night
Or washed thy garments in the stream;
To whose white bed had come the dream
That He was thine and thou wast His
Who feeds among the field-lilies.
O solemn shadow of the end
In that wise spirit long contain'd!
O awful end! and those unsaid
Long years when It was Finishèd!

Mind'st thou not (when the twilight gone
Left darkness in the house of John,)
Between the naked window-bars
That spacious vigil of the stars? –
For thou, a watcher even as they,
Wouldst rise from where throughout the day
Thou wroughtest raiment for His poor;
And, finding the fixed terms endure
Of day and night which never brought
Sounds of His coming chariot,
Wouldst lift through cloud-waste unexplor'd
Those eyes which said, "How long, O Lord?"
Then that disciple whom He loved,
Well heeding, haply would be moved
To ask thy blessing in His name;
And that one thought in both, the same
Though silent, then would clasp ye round
To weep together, – tears long bound,

Sick tears of patience, dumb and slow.
Yet, "Surely I come quickly," – so
He said, from life and death gone home.
Amen: even so, Lord Jesus, come!

But oh! what human tongue can speak
That day when Michael came[1] to break
From the tir'd spirit, like a veil,
Its covenant with Gabriel
Endured at length unto the end?
What human thought can apprehend
That mystery of motherhood
When thy Beloved at length renew'd
The sweet communion severèd, –
His left hand underneath thine head
And His right hand embracing thee? –
Lo! He was thine, and this is He!

Soul, is it Faith, or Love, or Hope,
That lets me see her standing up
Where the light of the Throne is bright?
Unto the left, unto the right,
The cherubim, succinct, conjoint,
Float inward to a golden point,
And from between the seraphim
The glory issues for a hymn.
O Mary Mother, be not loth
To listen, – thou whom the stars clothe,
Who seëst and mayst not be seen!
Hear us at last, O Mary Queen!
Into our shadow bend thy face,
Bowing thee from the secret place,
O Mary Virgin, full of grace!

[1] A Church legend of the Blessed Virgin's death.

The Portrait

This is her picture as she was:
  It seems a thing to wonder on,
As though mine image in the glass
  Should tarry when myself am gone.
I gaze until she seems to stir, –
Until mine eyes almost aver
  That now, even now, the sweet lips part
  To breathe the words of the sweet heart: –
And yet the earth is over her.

Alas! even such the thin-drawn ray
  That makes the prison-depths more rude, –
The drip of water night and day
  Giving a tongue to solitude.
Yet only this, of love's whole prize,
Remains; save what in mournful guise
  Takes counsel with my soul alone, –
  Save what is secret and unknown,
Below the earth, above the skies.

In painting her I shrined her face
  'Mid mystic trees, where light falls in
Hardly at all; a covert place
  Where you might think to find a din
Of doubtful talk, and a live flame
Wandering, and many a shape whose name
  Not itself knoweth, and old dew,
  And your own footsteps meeting you,
And all things going as they came.

A deep dim wood; and there she stands
  As in that wood that day: for so
Was the still movement of her hands
  And such the pure line's gracious flow.
And passing fair the type must seem,
Unknown the presence and the dream.

'Tis she: though of herself, alas!
Less than her shadow on the grass
Or than her image in the stream.

That day we met there, I and she
    One with the other all alone;
And we were blithe; yet memory
    Saddens those hours, as when the moon
Looks upon daylight. And with her
I stooped to drink the spring-water,
    Athirst where other waters sprang:
    And where the echo is, she sang, –
My soul another echo there.

But when that hour my soul won strength
    For words whose silence wastes and kills,
Dull raindrops smote us, and at length
    Thundered the heat within the hills.
That eve I spoke those words again
Beside the pelted window-pane;
    And there she hearkened what I said,
    With under-glances that surveyed
The empty pastures blind with rain.

Next day the memories of these things,
    Like leaves through which a bird has flown,
Still vibrated with Love's warm wings;
    Till I must make them all my own
And paint this picture. So, 'twixt ease
Of talk and sweet long silences,
    She stood among the plants in bloom
    At windows of a summer room,
To feign the shadow of the trees.

And as I wrought, while all above
    And all around was fragrant air,
In the sick burthen of my love
    It seemed each sun-thrilled blossom there

Beat like a heart among the leaves.
O heart that never beats nor heaves,
    In that one darkness lying still,
    What now to thee my love's great will
Or the fine web of the sunshine weaves?

For now doth daylight disavow
    Those days – nought left to see or hear.
Only in solemn whispers now
    At night-time these things reach mine ear;
When the leaf-shadows at a breath
Shrink in the road, and all the heath,
    Forest and water, far and wide,
    In limpid starlight glorified,
Lie like the mystery of death.

Last night at last I could have slept,
    And yet delayed my sleep till dawn,
Still wandering. Then it was I wept:
    For unawares I came upon
Those glades where once she walked with me:
And as I stood there suddenly,
    All wan with traversing the night,
    Upon the desolate verge of light
Yearned loud the iron-bosomed sea.

Even so, where Heaven holds breath and hears
    The beating heart of Love's own breast, –
Where round the secret of all spheres
    All angels lay their wings to rest, –
How shall my soul stand rapt and awed,
When, by the new birth borne abroad
    Throughout the music of the suns,
    It enters in her soul at once
And knows the silence there for God!

Here with her face doth memory sit
    Meanwhile, and wait the day's decline,
Till other eyes shall look from it,
    Eyes of the spirit's Palestine,
Even than the old gaze tenderer:
While hopes and aims long lost with her
    Stand round her image side by side,
    Like tombs of pilgrims that have died
About the Holy Sepulchre.

The Card-Dealer

Could you not drink her gaze like wine?
    Yet though its splendour swoon
Into the silence languidly
    As a tune into a tune,
Those eyes unravel the coiled night
    And know the stars at noon.

The gold that's heaped beside her hand,
    In truth rich prize it were;
And rich the dreams that wreathe her brows
    With magic stillness there;
And he were rich who should unwind
    That woven golden hair.

Around her, where she sits, the dance
    Now breathes its eager heat;
And not more lightly or more true
    Fall there the dancers' feet
Than fall her cards on the bright board
    As 'twere a heart that beat.

Her fingers let them softly through,
　　Smooth polished silent things;
And each one as it falls reflects
　　In swift light-shadowings,
Blood-red and purple, green and blue,
　　The great eyes of her rings.

Whom plays she with? With thee, who lov'st
　　Those gems upon her hand;
With me, who search her secret brows;
　　With all men, bless'd or bann'd.
We play together, she and we,
　　Within a vain strange land:

A land without any order, –
　　Day even as night, (one saith,) –
Where who lieth down ariseth not
　　Nor the sleeper awakeneth;
A land of darkness as darkness itself
　　And of the shadow of death.

What be her cards, you ask? Even these: –
　　The heart, that doth but crave
More, having fed; the diamond,
　　Skilled to make base seem brave;
The club, for smiting in the dark;
　　The spade, to dig a grave.

And do you ask what game she plays?
　　With me 'tis lost or won;
With thee it is playing still; with him
　　It is not well begun;
But 'tis a game she plays with all
　　Beneath the sway o' the sun.

Thou seest the card that falls, – she knows
  The card that followeth:
Her game in thy tongue is called Life,
  As ebbs thy daily breath:
When she shall speak, thou'lt learn her tongue
  And know she calls it Death.

Jenny

*Vengeance of Jenny's case! Fie on her! Never name
her, child!* – (Mrs Quickly.)

Lazy laughing languid Jenny,
Fond of a kiss and fond of a guinea,
Whose head upon my knee to-night
Rests for a while, as if grown light
With all our dances and the sound
To which the wild tunes spun you round:
Fair Jenny mine, the thoughtless queen
Of kisses which the blush between
Could hardly make much daintier;
Whose eyes are as blue skies, whose hair
Is countless gold incomparable:
Fresh flower, scarce touched with signs that tell
Of Love's exuberant hotbed: – Nay,
Poor flower left torn since yesterday
Until to-morrow leave you bare;
Poor handful of bright spring-water
Flung in the whirlpool's shrieking face;
Poor shameful Jenny, full of grace
Thus with your head upon my knee; –
Whose person or whose purse may be
The lodestar of your reverie?

This room of yours, my Jenny, looks
A change from mine so full of books,
Whose serried ranks hold fast, forsooth,
So many captive hours of youth, –
The hours they thieve from day and night
To make one's cherished work come right,
And leave it wrong for all their theft,
Even as to-night my work was left:
Until I vowed that since my brain
And eyes of dancing seemed so fain,
My feet should have some dancing too: –
And thus it was I met with you.
Well, I suppose 'twas hard to part,
For here I am. And now, sweetheart,
You seem too tired to get to bed.

It was a careless life I led
When rooms like this were scarce so strange
Not long ago. What breeds the change, –
The many aims or the few years?
Because to-night it all appears
Something I do not know again.

The cloud's not danced out of my brain, –
The cloud that made it turn and swim
While hour by hour the books grew dim.
Why, Jenny, as I watch you there, –
For all your wealth of loosened hair,
Your silk ungirdled and unlac'd
And warm sweets open to the waist,
All golden in the lamplight's gleam, –
You know not what a book you seem,
Half-read by lightning in a dream!
How should you know, my Jenny? Nay,
And I should be ashamed to say: –
Poor beauty, so well worth a kiss!
But while my thought runs on like this
With wasteful whims more than enough,
I wonder what you're thinking of.

If of myself you think at all,
What is the thought? – conjectural
On sorry matters best unsolved? –
Or inly is each grace revolved
To fit me with a lure? – or (sad
To think!) perhaps you're merely glad
That I'm not drunk or ruffianly
And let you rest upon my knee.

For sometimes, were the truth confess'd,
You're thankful for a little rest, –
Glad from the crush to rest within,
From the heart-sickness and the din
Where envy's voice at virtue's pitch
Mocks you because your gown is rich;
And from the pale girl's dumb rebuke,
Whose ill-clad grace and toil-worn look
Proclaim the strength that keeps her weak,
And other nights than yours bespeak;
And from the wise unchildish elf,
To schoolmate lesser than himself
Pointing you out, what thing you are: –
Yes, from the daily jeer and jar,
From shame and shame's outbraving too,
Is rest not sometimes sweet to you? –
But most from the hatefulness of man,
Who spares not to end what he began,
Whose acts are ill and his speech ill,
Who, having used you at his will,
Thrusts you aside, as when I dine
I serve the dishes and the wine.

Well, handsome Jenny mine, sit up:
I've filled our glasses, let us sup,
And do not let me think of you,
Lest shame of yours suffice for two.
What, still so tired? Well, well then, keep
Your head there, so you do not sleep;

But that the weariness may pass
And leave you merry, take this glass.
Ah! lazy lily hand, more bless'd
If ne'er in rings it had been dress'd
Nor ever by a glove conceal'd!

Behold the lilies of the field,
They toil not neither do they spin;
(So doth the ancient text begin, –
Not of such rest as one of these
Can share.) Another rest and ease
Along each summer-sated path
From its new lord the garden hath,
Than that whose spring in blessings ran
Which praised the bounteous husbandman,
Ere yet, in days of hankering breath,
The lilies sickened unto death.

What, Jenny, are your lilies dead?
Aye, and the snow-white leaves are spread
Like winter on the garden-bed.
But you had roses left in May, –
They were not gone too. Jenny, nay,
But must your roses die, and those
Their purfled buds that should unclose?
Even so; the leaves are curled apart,
Still red as from the broken heart,
And here's the naked stem of thorns.

Nay, nay, mere words. Here nothing warns
As yet of winter. Sickness here
Or want alone could waken fear, –
Nothing but passion wrings a tear.
Except when there may rise unsought
Haply at times a passing thought
Of the old days which seem to be
Much older than any history
That is written in any book;

When she would lie in fields and look
Along the ground through the blown grass,
And wonder where the city was,
Far out of sight, whose broil and bale
They told her then for a child's tale.

Jenny, you know the city now.
A child can tell the tale there, how
Some things which are not yet enroll'd
In market-lists are bought and sold
Even till the early Sunday light,
When Saturday night is market-night
Everywhere, be it dry or wet,
And market-night in the Haymarket.
Our learned London children know,
Poor Jenny, all your pride and woe;
Have seen your lifted silken skirt
Advertise dainties through the dirt;
Have seen your coach-wheels splash rebuke
On virtue; and have learned your look
When, wealth and health slipped past, you stare
Along the streets alone, and there,
Round the long park, across the bridge,
The cold lamps at the pavement's edge
Wind on together and apart,
A fiery serpent for your heart.

Let the thoughts pass, an empty cloud!
Suppose I were to think aloud, –
What if to her all this were said?
Why, as a volume seldom read
Being opened halfway shuts again,
So might the pages of her brain
Be parted at such words, and thence
Close back upon the dusty sense.
For is there hue or shape defin'd
In Jenny's desecrated mind,
Where all contagious currents meet,

A Lethe of the middle street?
Nay, it reflects not any face,
Nor sound is in its sluggish pace,
But as they coil those eddies clot,
And night and day remember not.

Why, Jenny, you're asleep at last! –
Asleep, poor Jenny, hard and fast, –
So young and soft and tired; so fair,
With chin thus nestled in your hair,
Mouth quiet, eyelids almost blue
As if some sky of dreams shone through!

Just as another woman sleeps!
Enough to throw one's thoughts in heaps
Of doubt and horror, – what to say
Or think, – this awful secret sway,
The potter's power over the clay!
Of the same lump (it has been said)
For honour and dishonour made,
Two sister vessels. Here is one.

My cousin Nell is fond of fun,
And fond of dress, and change, and praise,
So mere a woman in her ways:
And if her sweet eyes rich in youth
Are like her lips that tell the truth,
My cousin Nell is fond of love.
And she's the girl I'm proudest of.
Who does not prize her, guard her well?
The love of change, in cousin Nell,
Shall find the best and hold it dear:
The unconquered mirth turn quieter
Not through her own, through others' woe:
The conscious pride of beauty glow
Beside another's pride in her,
One little part of all they share.
For Love himself shall ripen these

In a kind soil to just increase
Through years of fertilizing peace.

Of the same lump (as it is said)
For honour and dishonour made,
Two sister vessels. Here is one.

It makes a goblin of the sun.

So pure, – so fall'n! How dare to think
Of the first common kindred link?
Yet, Jenny, till the world shall burn
It seems that all things take their turn;
And who shall say but this fair tree
May need, in changes that may be,
Your children's children's charity?
Scorned then, no doubt, as you are scorn'd!
Shall no man hold his pride forewarn'd
Till in the end, the Day of Days,
At Judgment, one of his own race,
As frail and lost as you, shall rise, –
His daughter, with his mother's eyes?

How Jenny's clock ticks on the shelf!
Might not the dial scorn itself
That has such hours to register?
Yet as to me, even so to her
Are golden sun and silver moon,
In daily largesse of earth's boon,
Counted for life-coins to one tune.
And if, as blindfold fates are toss'd,
Through some one man this life be lost,
Shall soul not somehow pay for soul?

Fair shines the gilded aureole
In which our highest painters place
Some living woman's simple face.
And the stilled features thus descried

As Jenny's long throat droops aside, –
The shadows where the cheeks are thin,
And pure wide curve from ear to chin, –
With Raffael's, Leonardo's hand
To show them to men's souls, might stand,
Whole ages long, the whole world through,
For preachings of what God can do.
What has man done here? How atone,
Great God, for this which man has done?
And for the body and soul which by
Man's pitiless doom must now comply
With lifelong hell, what lullaby
Of sweet forgetful second birth
Remains? All dark. No sign on earth
What measure of God's rest endows
The many mansions of his house.

    If but a woman's heart might see
Such erring heart unerringly
For once! But that can never be.

    Like a rose shut in a book
In which pure women may not look,
For its base pages claim control
To crush the flower within the soul;
Where though each dead rose-leaf that clings,
Pale as transparent Psyche-wings,
To the vile text, are traced such things
As might make lady's cheek indeed
More than a living rose to read;
So nought save foolish foulness may
Watch with hard eyes the sure decay;
And so the life-blood of this rose,
Puddled with shameful knowledge, flows
Through leaves no chaste hand may unclose:
Yet still it keeps such faded show
Of when 'twas gathered long ago,
That the crushed petals' lovely grain,

The sweetness of the sanguine stain,
Seen of a woman's eyes, must make
Her pitiful heart, so prone to ache,
Love roses better for its sake: –
Only that this can never be: –
Even so unto her sex is she.

Yet, Jenny, looking long at you,
The woman almost fades from view.
A cipher of man's changeless sum
Of lust, past, present, and to come,
Is left. A riddle that one shrinks
To challenge from the scornful sphinx.

Like a toad within a stone
Seated while Time crumbles on;
Which sits there since the earth was curs'd
For Man's transgression at the first;
Which, living through all centuries,
Not once has seen the sun arise;
Whose life, to its cold circle charmed,
The earth's whole summers have not warmed;
Which always – whitherso the stone
Be flung – sits there, deaf, blind, alone; –
Aye, and shall not be driven out
Till that which shuts him round about
Break at the very Master's stroke,
And the dust thereof vanish as smoke,
And the seed of Man vanish as dust: –
Even so within this world is Lust.

Come, come, what use in thoughts like this?
Poor little Jenny, good to kiss, –
You'd not believe by what strange roads
Thought travels, when your beauty goads
A man to-night to think of toads!
Jenny, wake up.... Why, there's the dawn!

And there's an early waggon drawn
To market, and some sheep that jog
Bleating before a barking dog;
And the old streets come peering through
Another night that London knew;
And all as ghostlike as the lamps.

So on the wings of day decamps
My last night's frolic. Glooms begin
To shiver off as lights creep in
Past the gauze curtains half drawn-to,
And the lamp's doubled shade grows blue, –
Your lamp, my Jenny, kept alight,
Like a wise virgin's, all one night!
And in the alcove coolly spread
Glimmers with dawn your empty bed;
And yonder your fair face I see
Reflected lying on my knee,
Where teems with first foreshadowings
Your pier-glass scrawled with diamond rings:
And on your bosom all night worn
Yesterday's rose now droops forlorn,
But dies not yet this summer morn.

And now without, as if some word
Had called upon them that they heard,
The London sparrows far and nigh
Clamour together suddenly;
And Jenny's cage-bird grown awake
Here in their song his part must take,
Because here too the day doth break.

And somehow in myself the dawn
Among stirred clouds and veils withdrawn
Strikes greyly on her. Let her sleep.
But will it wake her if I heap
These cushions thus beneath her head
Where my knee was? No, – there's your bed,

My Jenny, while you dream. And there
I lay among your golden hair
Perhaps the subject of your dreams,
These golden coins.

                For still one deems
That Jenny's flattering sleep confers
New magic on the magic purse, –
Grim web, how clogged with shrivelled flies!
Between the threads fine fumes arise
And shape their pictures in the brain.
There roll no streets in glare and rain,
Nor flagrant man-swine whets his tusk;
But delicately sighs in musk
The homage of the dim boudoir;
Or like a palpitating star
Thrilled into song, the opera-night
Breathes faint in the quick pulse of light;
Or at the carriage-window shine
Rich wares for choice; or, free to dine,
Whirls through its hour of health (divine
For her) the concourse of the Park.
And though in the discounted dark
Her functions here and here are one,
Beneath the lamps and in the sun
There reigns at least the acknowledged belle
Apparelled beyond parallel.
Ah Jenny, yes, we know your dreams.

For even the Paphian Venus seems
A goddess o'er the realms of love,
When silver-shrined in shadowy grove:
Aye, or let offerings nicely plac'd
But hide Pripaus to the waist,
And whoso looks on him shall see
An eligible deity.

Why, Jenny, waking here along
May help you to remember one,

Though all the memory's long outworn
Of many a double-pillowed morn.
I think I see you when you wake,
And rub your eyes for me, and shake
My gold, in rising, from your hair,
A Danaë for a moment there.

Jenny, my love rang true! for still
Love at first sight is vague, until
That tinkling makes him audible.

And must I mock you to the last,
Ashamed of my own shame, – aghast
Because some thoughts not born amiss
Rose at a poor fair face like this?
Well, of such thoughts so much I know:
In my life, as in hers, they show,
By a far gleam which I may near,
A dark path I can strive to clear.

Only one kiss. Good-bye, my dear.

A Trip to Paris and Belgium

I *London to Folkestone*

A constant keeping-past of shaken trees,
And a bewildered glitter of loose road;
Banks of bright growth, with single blades atop
Against white sky: and wires – a constant chain –
That seem to draw the clouds along with them
(Things which one stoops against the light to see
Through the low window; shaking by at rest,
Or fierce like water as the swiftness grows);
And, seen through fences or a bridge far off,

Trees that in moving keep their intervals
Still one 'twixt bar and bar; and then at times
Long reaches of green level, where one cow,
Feeding among her fellows that feed on,
Lifts her slow neck, and gazes for the sound.

Fields mown in ridges; and close garden-crops
Of the earth's increase; and a constant sky
Still with clear trees that let you see the wind;
And snatches of the engine-smoke, by fits
Tossed to the wind against the landscape, where
Rooks stooping heave their wings upon the day.

Brick walls we pass between, passed so at once
That for the suddenness I cannot know
Or what, or where begun, or where at end.
Sometimes a station in grey quiet; whence,
With a short gathered champing of pent sound,
We are let out upon the air again.
Pauses of water soon, at intervals,
That has the sky in it; – the reflexes
O' the trees move towards the bank as we go by,
Leaving the water's surface plain. I now
Lie back and close my eyes a space; for they
Smart from the open forwardness of thought
Fronting the wind.

*   *   *

I did not scribble more,
Be certain, after this; but yawned, and read,
And nearly dozed a little, I believe;
Till, stretching up against the carriage-back,
I was roused altogether, and looked out
To where the pale sea brooded murmuring.

70

II *Boulogne to Amiens and Paris*

Strong extreme speed, that the brain hurries with,
Further than trees, and hedges, and green grass
Whitened by distance, – further than small pools
Held among fields and gardens, further than
Haystacks, and wind-mill-sails, and roofs and herds, –
The sea's last margin ceases at the sun.

The sea has left us, but the sun remains.
Sometimes the country spreads aloof in tracts
Smooth from the harvest; sometimes sky and land
Are shut from the square space the window leaves
By a dense crowd of trees, stem behind stem
Passing across each other as we pass:
Sometimes tall poplar-wands stand white, their heads
Outmeasuring the distant hills. Sometimes
The ground has a deep greenness; sometimes brown
In stubble; and sometimes no ground at all,
For the close strength of crops that stand unreaped.
The water-plots are sometimes all the sun's, –
Sometimes quite green through shadows filling them,
Or islanded with growths of reeds, – or else
Masked in green dust like the wide face o' the fields.
And still the swiftness lasts; that to our speed
The trees seem shaken like a press of spears.

There is some count of us: – folks travelling-capped,
Priesthood, and lank hard-featured soldiery,
Females (no women), blouses, Hunt, and I.

We are relayed at Amiens. The steam
Snorts, chafes, and bridles, like three hundred horse,
And flings its dusky mane upon the air.
Our company is thinned, and lamps alight:
But still there are the folks in travelling-caps –
No priesthood now, but always soldiery,
And babies to make up for show in noise;
Females (no women), blouses, Hunt, and I.

71

Our windows at one side are shut for warmth;
Upon the other side, a leaden sky,
Hung in blank glare, makes all the country dim,
Which too seems bald and meagre, – be it truth,
Or of the waxing darkness. Here and there
The shade takes light, where in thin patches stand
The unstirred dregs of water.

III   *The Paris Railway-Station*

In France (to baffle thieves and murderers)
A journey takes two days of passport work
At least. The plan's sometimes a tedious one,
But bears its fruit. Because, the other day,
In passing by the Morgue, we saw a man
(The thing is common, and we never should
Have known of it, only we passed that way)
Who had been stabbed and tumbled in the Seine,
Where he had stayed some days. The face was black,
And, like a negro's, swollen; all the flesh
Had furred, and broken into a green mould.

Now, very likely, he who did the job
Was standing among those who stood with us,
To look upon the corpse. You fancy him –
Smoking an early pipe, and watching, as
An artist, the effect of his last work.
This always if it had not struck him that
'Twere best to leave while yet the body took
Its crust of rot beneath the Seine. It may:
But, if it did not, he can now remain
Without much fear. *Only*, if he should want
To travel, and have not his passport yet,
(Deep dogs these French police!) he may be caught.

Therefore you see (lest, being murderers,
We should not have the sense to go before

The thing were known, or to stay afterwards)
There is good reason why – having resolved
To start for Belgium – we were kept three days
To learn about the passports first, then do
As we had learned. This notwithstanding, in
The fulness of the time 'tis come to pass.

IV   *Reaching Brussels*

There is small change of country; but the sun
Is out, and it seems shame this were not said.
For upon all the grass the warmth has caught;
And betwixt distant whitened poplar-stems
Makes greener darkness; and in dells of trees
Shows spaces of a verdure that was hid;
And the sky has its blue floated with white,
And crossed with falls of the sun's glory aslant
To lay upon the waters of the world;
And from the road men stand with shaded eyes
To look; and flowers in gardens have grown strong,
And our own shadows here within the coach
Are brighter; and all colour has more bloom.

So, after the sore torments of the route: –
Toothache, and headache, and the ache of wind,
And huddled sleep, and smarting wakefulness,
And night, and day, and hunger sick at food,
And twenty-fold relays, and packages
To be unlocked, and passports to be found,
And heavy well-kept landscape; – we were glad
Because we entered Brussels in the sun.

V   *Antwerp to Ghent*

We are upon the Scheldt. We know we move
Because there is a floating at our eyes
Whatso they seek; and because all the things
Which on our outset were distinct and large

73

Are smaller and much weaker and quite grey,
And at last gone from us. No motion else.

We are upon the road. The thin swift moon
Runs with the running clouds that are the sky,
And with the running water runs – at whiles
Weak 'neath the film and heavy growth of reeds.
The country swims with motion. Time itself
Is consciously beside us, and perceived.
Our speed is such the sparks our engine leaves
Are burning after the whole train has passed.
The darkness is a tumult. We tear on,
The roll behind us and the cry before,
Constantly, in a lull of intense speed
And thunder. Any other sound is known
Merely by sight. The shrubs, the trees your eye
Scans for their growth, are far along in haze.
The sky has lost its clouds, and lies away
Oppressively at calm: the moon has failed:
Our speed has set the wind against us. Now
Our engine's heat is fiercer, and flings up
Great glares alongside. Wind and steam and speed
And clamour and the night. We are in Ghent.

Near Brussels – A Half-way Pause

The turn of noontide has begun.
    In the weak breeze the sunshine yields.
    There is a bell upon the fields.
On the long hedgerow's tangled run
    A low white cottage intervenes:
    Against the wall a blind man leans,
And sways his face to have the sun.

Our horses' hoofs stir in the road,
    Quiet and sharp. Light hath a song

Whose silence, being heard, seems long.
The point of noon maketh abode,
   And will not be at once gone through.
   The sky's deep colour saddens you,
And the heat weighs a dreamy load.

Antwerp and Bruges

I climbed the stair in Antwerp church,
   What time the circling thews of sound
   At sunset seem to heave it round.
Far up, the carillon did search
The wind, and the birds came to perch
   Far under, where the gables wound.

In Antwerp harbour on the Scheldt
   I stood along, a certain space
   Of night. The mist was near my face;
Deep on, the flow was heard and felt.
The carillon kept pause, and dwelt
   In music through the silent place.

John Memmeling and John van Eyck
   Hold state at Bruges. In sore shame
   I scanned the works that keep their name.
The carillon, which then did strike
Mine ears, was heard of theirs alike:
   It set me closer unto them.

I climbed at Bruges all the flight
   The belfry has of ancient stone.
   For leagues I saw the east wind blown;
The earth was grey, the sky was white.
I stood so near upon the height
   That my flesh felt the carillon.

FOR
Our Lady of the Rocks
BY LEONARDO DA VINCI

Mother, is this the darkness of the end,
   The Shadow of Death? and is that outer sea
   Infinite imminent Eternity?
And does the death-pang by man's seed sustained
In Time's each instant cause thy face to bend
   Its silent prayer upon the Son, while He
   Blesses the dead with His hand silently
To His long day which hours no more offend?

Mother of grace, the pass is difficult,
   Keen as these rocks, and the bewildered souls
     Throng it like echoes, blindly shuddering through.
   Thy name, O Lord, each spirit's voice extols,
     Whose peace abides in the dark avenue
Amid the bitterness of things occult.

FOR
A Venetian Pastoral
BY GIORGIONE
(In the Louvre)

Water, for anguish of the solstice: – nay,
   But dip the vessel slowly, – nay, but lean
   And hark how at its verge the wave sighs in
Reluctant. Hush! beyond all depth away
The heat lies silent at the brink of day:
   Now the hand trails upon the viol-string
   That sobs, and the brown faces cease to sing,
Sad with the whole of pleasure. Whither stray
Her eyes now, from whose mouth the slim pipes creep
   And leave it pouting, while the shadowed grass
     Is cool against her naked side? Let be: –

Say nothing now unto her lest she weep,
  Nor name this ever. Be it as it was, –
    Life touching lips with Immortality.

An Allegorical Dance of Women
BY ANDREA MANTEGNA
(In the Louvre)

Scarcely, I think; yet it indeed *may* be
  The meaning reached him, when this music rang
  Clear through his frame, a sweet possessive pang,
And he beheld these rocks and that ridged sea.
But I believe that, leaning tow'rds them, he
  Just felt their hair carried across his face
  As each girl passed him; nor gave ear to trace
How many feet; nor bent assuredly
His eyes from the blind fixedness of thought
  To know the dancers. It is bitter glad
    Even unto tears. Its meaning filleth it,
    A secret of the wells of Life: to wit: –
The heart's each pulse shall keep the sense it had
With all, though the mind's labour run to nought.

FOR
Ruggiero and Angelica
BY INGRES

I

A remote sky, prolonged to the sea's brim:
  One rock-point standing buffeted alone,
  Vexed at its base with a foul beast unknown,
Hell-birth of geomaunt and teraphim:

A knight, and a winged creature bearing him,
   Reared at the rock: a woman fettered there,
   Leaning into the hollow with loose hair
And throat let back and heartsick trail of limb.

The sky is harsh, and the sea shrewd and salt:
   Under his lord the griffin-horse ramps blind
     With rigid wings and tail. The spear's lithe stem
   Thrills in the roaring of those jaws: behind,
That evil length of body chafes at fault.
     She does not hear nor see – she knows of them.

II

Clench thine eyes now, – 'tis the last instant, girl:
   Draw in thy senses, set thy knees, and take
   One breath for all: thy life is keen awake, –
Thou mayst not swoon. Was that the scattered whirl
Of its foam drenched thee? – or the waves that curl
   And split, bleak spray wherein thy temples ache?
   Or was it his the champion's blood to flake
Thy flesh? – or thine own blood's anointing, girl?

Now, silence: for the sea's is such a sound
   As irks not silence; and except the sea,
     All now is still. Now the dead thing doth cease
To writhe, and drifts. He turns to her: and she,
Cast from the jaws of Death, remains there, bound,
   Again a woman in her nakedness.

A Virgin and Child
BY HANS MEMMELINCK
(In the Academy of Bruges)

Mystery: God, man's life, born into man
   Of woman. There abideth on her brow
   The ended pang of knowledge, the which now
Is calm assured. Since first her task began
She hath known all. What more of anguish than
   Endurance oft hath lived through, the whole space
   Through night till day, passed weak upon her face
While the heard lapse of darkness slowly ran?

All hath been told her touching her dear Son,
   And all shall be accomplished. Where He sits
    Even now, a babe, He holds the symbol fruit
   Perfect and chosen. Until God permits,
    His soul's elect still have the absolute
Harsh nether darkness, and make painful moan.

Sister Helen

"Why did you melt your waxen man,
                    Sister Helen?
To-day is the third since you began."
"The time was long, yet the time ran,
                    Little brother."
                    (*O Mother, Mary Mother,*
Three days to-day, between Hell and Heaven!)

"But if you have done your work aright,
                    Sister Helen,
You'll let me play, for you said I might."
"Be very still in your play to-night,
                    Little brother."
                    (*O Mother, Mary Mother,*
Third night, to-night, between Hell and Heaven!)

"You said it must melt ere vesper-bell,
                    Sister Helen;
If now it be molten, all is well."
"Even so, – nay, peace! you cannot tell,
                    Little brother."
                    (*O Mother, Mary Mother,*
O what is this, between Hell and Heaven?)

"Oh the waxen knave was plump to-day,
                    Sister Helen;
How like dead folk he has dropped away!"
"Nay now, of the dead what can you say,
                    Little brother?"
                    (*O Mother, Mary Mother,*
What of the dead, between Hell and Heaven?)

"See, see, the sunken pile of wood,
                    Sister Helen,
Shines through the thinned wax red as blood!"
"Nay now, when looked you yet on blood,
                    Little brother?"
                    (*O Mother, Mary Mother,*
How pale she is, between Hell and Heaven!)

"Now close your eyes, for they're sick and sore,
                    Sister Helen,
And I'll play without the gallery door."
"Aye, let me rest, – I'll lie on the floor,
                    Little brother."
                    (*O Mother, Mary Mother,*
What rest to-night, between Hell and Heaven?)

"Here high up in the balcony,
                    Sister Helen,
The moon flies face to face with me."
"Aye, look and say whatever you see,
                    Little brother."
                    (*O Mother, Mary Mother,*
What sight to-night, between Hell and Heaven?)

"Outside it's merry in the wind's wake,
                    Sister Helen;
In the shaken trees the chill stars shake."
"Hush, heard you a horse-tread as you spake,
                    Little brother?"
                    (*O Mother, Mary Mother,*
What sound to-night, between Hell and Heaven?)

"I hear a horse-tread, and I see,
                    Sister Helen,
Three horsemen that ride terribly."
"Little brother, whence come the three,
                    Little brother?"
                    (*O Mother, Mary Mother,*
Whence should they come, between Hell and Heaven?)

"They come by the hill-verge from Boyne Bar,
                    Sister Helen,
And one draws nigh, but two are afar."
"Look, look, do you know them who they are,
                    Little brother?"
                    (*O Mother, Mary Mother,*
Who should they be, between Hell and Heaven?)

"Oh, it's Keith of Eastholm rides so fast,
                    Sister Helen,
For I know the white mane on the blast."
"The hour has come, has come at last,
                    Little brother!"
                    (*O Mother, Mary Mother,*
Her hour at last, between Hell and Heaven!)

"He has made a sign and called Halloo!
                    Sister Helen,
And he says that he would speak with you."
"Oh tell him I fear the frozen dew,
                    Little brother."
                    (*O Mother, Mary Mother,*
Why laughs she thus, between Hell and Heaven?)

"The wind is loud, but I hear him cry,
                    Sister Helen,
That Keith of Ewern's like to die."
"And he and thou, and thou and I,
                    Little brother."
                    (*O Mother, Mary Mother,*
And they and we, between Hell and Heaven!)

"Three days ago, on his marriage-morn,
                    Sister Helen,
He sickened, and lies since then forlorn."
"For bridegroom's side is the bride a thorn,
                    Little brother?"
                    (*O Mother, Mary Mother,*
Cold bridal cheer, between Hell and Heaven!)

"Three days and nights he has lain abed,
                    Sister Helen,
And he prays in torment to be dead."
"The thing may chance, if he have prayed,
                    Little brother!"
                    (*O Mother, Mary Mother,*
If he have prayed, between Hell and Heaven!)

"But he has not ceased to cry to-day,
                    Sister Helen,
That you should take your curse away."
"My prayer was heard, – he need but pray,
                    Little brother!"
                    (*O Mother, Mary Mother,*
Shall God not hear, between Hell and Heaven?)

"But he says, till you take back your ban,
                    Sister Helen,
His soul would pass, yet never can."
"Nay then, shall I slay a living man,
                    Little brother?"
                    (*O Mother, Mary Mother,*
A living soul, between Hell and Heaven!)

"But he calls for ever on your name,
                    Sister Helen,
And says that he melts before a flame."
"My heart for his pleasure fared the same,
                    Little brother."
                    (*O Mother, Mary Mother,*
Fire at the heart, between Hell and Heaven!)

"Here's Keith of Westholm riding fast,
                    Sister Helen,
For I know the white plume on the blast."
"The hour, the sweet hour I forecast,
                    Little brother!"
                    (*O Mother, Mary Mother,*
Is the hour sweet, between Hell and Heaven?)

"He stops to speak, and he stills his horse,
                    Sister Helen;
But his words are drowned in the wind's course."
"Nay hear, nay hear, you must hear perforce,
                    Little brother!"
                    (*O Mother, Mary Mother,*
What word now heard, between Hell and Heaven?)

"Oh he says that Keith of Ewern's cry,
                    Sister Helen,
Is ever to see you ere he die."
"In all that his soul sees, there am I,
                    Little brother!"
                    (*O Mother, Mary Mother,*
The soul's one sight, between Hell and Heaven!)

"He sends a ring and a broken coin,
                    Sister Helen,
And bids you mind the banks of Boyne."
"What else he broke will he ever join,
                    Little brother?"
                    (*O Mother, Mary Mother,*
No, never joined, between Hell and Heaven!)

"He yields you these and craves full fain,
                    Sister Helen,
You pardon him in his mortal pain."
"What else he took will he give again,
                    Little brother?"
                    (*O Mother, Mary Mother,*
Not twice to give, between Hell and Heaven!)

"He calls your name in an agony,
                    Sister Helen,
That even dead Love must weep to see."
"Hate, born of Love, is blind as he,
                    Little brother!"
                    (*O Mother, Mary Mother,*
Love turned to hate, between Hell and Heaven!)

84

"Oh it's Keith of Keith now that rides fast,
                    Sister Helen,
For I know the white hair on the blast."
"The short short hour will soon be past,
                    Little brother!"
                    (*O Mother, Mary Mother,*
Will soon be past, between Hell and Heaven!)

"He looks at me and he tries to speak,
                    Sister Helen,
But oh! his voice is sad and weak!"
"What here should the mighty Baron seek,
                    Little brother?"
                    (*O Mother, Mary Mother,*
Is this the end, between Hell and Heaven?)

"Oh his son still cries, if you forgive,
                    Sister Helen,
The body dies but the soul shall live."
"Fire shall forgive me as I forgive,
                    Little brother!"
                    (*O Mother, Mary Mother,*
As she forgives, between Hell and Heaven!)

"Oh he prays you, as his heart would rive,
                    Sister Helen,
To save his dear son's soul alive."
"Fire cannot slay it, it shall thrive,
                    Little brother!"
                    (*O Mother, Mary Mother,*
Alas, alas, between Hell and Heaven!)

"He cries to you, kneeling in the road,
                    Sister Helen,
To go with him for the love of God!"
"The way is long to his son's abode,
                    Little brother."
                    (*O Mother, Mary Mother,*
The way is long, between Hell and Heaven!)

"A lady's here, by a dark steed brought,
                    Sister Helen,
So darkly clad, I saw her not."
"See her now or never see aught,
                    Little brother!"
                    (*O Mother, Mary Mother,*
What more to see, between Hell and Heaven?)

"Her hood falls back, and the moon shines fair,
                    Sister Helen,
On the Lady of Ewern's golden hair."
"Blest hour of my power and her despair,
                    Little brother!"
                    (*O Mother, Mary Mother,*
Hour blest and bann'd, between Hell and Heaven!)

"Pale, pale her cheeks, that in pride did glow,
                    Sister Helen,
'Neath the bridal-wreath three days ago."
"One morn for pride and three days for woe,
                    Little brother!"
                    (*O Mother, Mary Mother,*
Three days, three nights, between Hell and Heaven!)

"Her clasped hands stretch from her bending head,
                    Sister Helen;
With the loud wind's wail her sobs are wed."
"What wedding-strains hath her bridal-bed,
                    Little brother?"
                    (*O Mother, Mary Mother,*
What strain but death's, between Hell and Heaven!)

"She may not speak, she sinks in a swoon,
                    Sister Helen, –
She lifts her lips and gasps on the moon."
"Oh! might I but hear her soul's blithe tune,
                    Little brother!"
                    (*O Mother, Mary Mother,*
Her woe's dumb cry, between Hell and Heaven!)

"They've caught her to Westholm's saddle-bow,
                    Sister Helen,
And her moonlit hair gleams white in its flow."
"Let it turn whiter than winter snow,
                    Little brother!"
                    (*O Mother, Mary Mother,*
Woe-withered gold, between Hell and Heaven!)

"O Sister Helen, you heard the bell,
                    Sister Helen!
More loud than the vesper-chime it fell."
"No vesper-chime, but a dying knell,
                    Little brother!"
                    (*O Mother, Mary Mother,*
His dying knell, between Hell and Heaven!)

"Alas! but I fear the heavy sound,
                    Sister Helen;
Is it in the sky or in the ground?"
"Say, have they turned their horses round,
                    Little brother?"
                    (*O Mother, Mary Mother,*
What would she more, between Hell and Heaven?)

"They have raised the old man from his knee,
                    Sister Helen,
And they ride in silence hastily."
"More fast the naked soul doth flee,
                    Little brother!"
                    (*O Mother, Mary Mother,*
The naked soul, between Hell and Heaven!)

"Flank to flank are the three steeds gone,
                    Sister Helen,
But the lady's dark steed goes alone."
"And lonely her bridegroom's soul hath flown,
                    Little brother."
                    (*O Mother, Mary Mother,*
The lonely ghost, between Hell and Heaven!)

"Oh the wind is sad in the iron chill,
                    Sister Helen,
And weary sad they look by the hill."
"But he and I are sadder still,
                    Little brother!"
                    (*O Mother, Mary Mother,*
Most sad of all, between Hell and Heaven!)

"See, see, the wax has dropped from its place,
                    Sister Helen,
And the flames are winning up apace!"
"Yet here they burn but for a space,
                    Little brother!"
                    (*O Mother, Mary Mother,*
Here for a space, between Hell and Heaven!)

"Ah! what white thing at the door has cross'd,
                    Sister Helen?
Ah! what is this that sighs in the frost?"
"A soul that's lost as mine is lost,
                    Little brother!"
                    (*O Mother, Mary Mother,*
Lost, lost, all lost, between Hell and Heaven!)

Dawn on the Night-Journey

Till dawn the wind drove round me. It is past
    And still, and leaves the air to lisp of bird,
    And to the quiet that is almost heard
Of the new-risen day, as yet bound fast
In the first warmth of sunrise. When the last
    Of the sun's hours to-day shall be fulfilled,
    There shall another breath of time be stilled
For me, which now is to my senses cast

As much beyond me as eternity,
   Unknown, kept secret. On the newborn air
      The moth quivers in silence. It is vast,
Yea, even beyond the hills upon the sea,
   The day whose end shall give this hour as sheer
      As chaos to the irrevocable Past.

A Young Fir-wood

These little firs today are things
   To clasp into a giant's cap,
   Or fans to suit his lady's lap.
From many winters many springs
   Shall cherish them in strength and sap
   Till they be marked upon the map,
A wood for the wind's wanderings.

All seed is in the sower's hands:
   And what at first was trained to spread
   Its shelter for some single head, –
Yea, even such fellowship of wands, –
   May hide the sunset, and the shade
   Of its great multitude be laid
Upon the earth and elder sands.

The Mirror

She knew it not: – most perfect pain
   To learn: this too she knew not. Strife
      For me, calm hers, as from the first.
      'Twas but another bubble burst
   Upon the curdling draught of life, –
My silent patience mine again.

89

As who, of forms that crowd unknown
   Within a distant mirror's shade,
     Deems such an one himself, and makes
     Some sign; but when the image shakes
   No whit, he finds his thought betray'd,
And must seek elsewhere for his own.

During Music

O cool unto the sense of pain
   That last night's sleep could not destroy;
   O warm unto the sense of joy,
That dreams its life within the brain.

What though I lean o'er thee to scan
   The written music cramped and stiff; –
   'Tis dark to me, as hieroglyph
On those weird bulks Egyptian.

But as from those, dumb now and strange,
   A glory wanders on the earth,
   Even so thy tones can call a birth
From these, to shake my soul with change.

O swift, as in melodious haste
   Float o'er the keys thy fingers small;
   O soft, as is the rise and fall
Which stirs that shade within thy breast.

The Honeysuckle

I plucked a honeysuckle where
   The hedge on high is quick with thorn,
   And climbing for the prize, was torn,
And fouled my feet in quag-water;
   And by the thorns and by the wind
   The blossom that I took was thinn'd,
And yet I found it sweet and fair.

Thence to a richer growth I came,
   Where, nursed in mellow intercourse,
   The honeysuckles sprang by scores,
Not harried like my single stem,
   All virgin lamps of scent and dew.
   So from my hand that first I threw,
Yet plucked not any more of them.

Sudden Light

I have been here before,
   But when or how I cannot tell:
I know the grass beyond the door,
   The sweet, keen smell,
The sighing sound, the lights around the shore.

You have been mine before, –
   How long ago I may not know:
But just when at that swallow's soar
   Your neck turned so,
Some veil did fall, – I knew it all of yore.

Has this been thus before?
   And shall not thus time's eddying flight
Still with our lives our love restore
   In death's despite,
And day and night yield one delight once more?

The Woodspurge

The wind flapped loose, the wind was still,
Shaken out dead from tree and hill:
I had walked on at the wind's will, –
I sat now, for the wind was still.

Between my knees my forehead was, –
My lips, drawn in, said not Alas!
My hair was over in the grass,
My naked ears heard the day pass.

My eyes, wide open, had the run
Of some ten weeds to fix upon;
Among those few, out of the sun,
The woodspurge flowered, three cups in one.

From perfect grief there need not be
Wisdom or even memory:
One thing then learnt remains to me, –
The woodspurge has a cup of three.

Even So

So it is, my dear.
All such things touch secret strings
For heavy hearts to hear.
So it is, my dear.

Very like indeed:
Sea and sky, afar, on high,
Sand and strewn seaweed, –
Very like indeed.

But the sea stands spread
As one wall with the flat skies,
Where the lean black craft like flies
    Seem well-nigh stagnated,
    Soon to drop off dead.

    Seemed it so to us
When I was thine and thou wast mine,
    And all these things were thus,
    But all our world in us?

    Could we be so now?
Not if all beneath heaven's pall
    Lay dead but I and thou,
    Could we be so now!

A Little While

A little while a little love
   The hour yet bears for thee and me
   Who have not drawn the veil to see
If still our heaven be lit above.
Thou merely, at the day's last sigh,
   Hast felt thy soul prolong the tone;
And I have heard the night-wind cry
    And deemed its speech mine own.

A little while a little love
   The scattering autumn hoards for us
   Whose bower is not yet ruinous
Nor quite unleaved our songless grove.
Only across the shaken boughs
   We hear the flood-tides seek the sea,
And deep in both our hearts they rouse
    One wail for thee and me.

A little while a little love
   May yet be ours who have not said
   The word it makes our eyes afraid
To know that each is thinking of.
Not yet the end: be our lips dumb
   In smiles a little season yet:
I'll tell thee, when the end is come,
   How we may best forget.

Sunset Wings

Tonight this sunset spreads two golden wings
   Cleaving the western sky;
Winged too with wind it is, and winnowings
Of birds; as if the day's last hour in rings
   Of strenuous flight must die.

Sun-steeped in fire, the homeward pinions sway
   Above the dovecote-tops;
And clouds of starlings, ere they rest with day,
Sink, clamorous like mill-waters, at wild play,
   By turns in every copse:

Each tree heart-deep the wrangling rout receives, –
   Save for the whirr within,
You could not tell the starlings from the leaves;
Then one great puff of wings, and the swarm heaves
   Away with all its din.

Even thus Hope's hours, in ever-eddying flight,
   To many a refuge tend;
With the first light she laughed, and the last light
Glows round her still; who natheless in the night
   At length must make an end.

And now the mustering rooks innumerable
   Together sail and soar,
While for the day's death, like a tolling knell,
Unto the heart they seem to cry, Farewell,
   No more, farewell, no more!

Is Hope not plumed, as 'twere a fiery dart?
   And oh! thou dying day,
Even as thou goest must she too depart,
And Sorrow fold such pinions on the heart
   As will not fly away?

Three Shadows

I looked and saw your eyes
   In the shadow of your hair
As a traveller sees the stream
   In the shadow of the wood;
And I said, "My faint heart sighs
   Ah me! to linger there,
To drink deep and to dream
   In that sweet solitude."

I looked and saw your heart
   In the shadow of your eyes,
As a seeker sees the gold
   In the shadow of the stream;
And I said, "Ah me! what art
   Should win the immortal prize,
Whose want must make life cold
   And Heaven a hollow dream?"

I looked and saw your love
   In the shadow of your heart,
As a diver sees the pearl
   In the shadow of the sea;
And I murmured, not above
   My breath, but all apart, –
"Ah! you can love, true girl,
   And is your love for me?"

Aspecta Medusa

Andromeda, by Perseus saved and wed,
Hankered each day to see the Gorgon's head:
Till o'er a fount he held it, bade her lean,
And mirrored in the wave was safely seen
That death she lived by.

              Let not thine eyes know
Any forbidden thing itself, although
It once should save as well as kill: but be
Its shadow upon life enough for thee.

Astarte Syriaca

Mystery: lo! betwixt the sun and moon
  Astarte of the Syrians: Venus Queen
  Ere Aphrodite was. In silver sheen
Her twofold girdle clasps the infinite boon
Of bliss whereof the heaven and earth commune:
  And from her neck's inclining flower-stem lean
  Love-freighted lips and absolute eyes that wean
The pulse of hearts to the spheres' dominant tune.

Torch-bearing, her sweet ministers compel
  All thrones of light beyond the sky and sea
  The witnesses of Beauty's face to be:
That face, of Love's all-penetrative spell
Amulet, talisman, and oracle, –
  Betwixt the sun and moon a mystery.

Spheral Change

In this new shade of Death, the show
  Passes me still of form and face;
Some bent, some gazing as they go,
  Some swiftly, some at a dull pace,
  Not one that speaks in any case.

If only one might speak! – the one
  Who never waits till I come near;
But always seated all alone
  As listening to the sunken air,
  Is gone before I come to her.

O dearest! while we lived and died
  A living death in every day,
Some hours we still were side by side,
  When where I was you too might stay
  And rest and need not go away.

O nearest, furthest! Can there be
  At length some hard-earned heart-won home,
Where, – exile changed for sanctuary, –
  Our lot may fill indeed its sum,
  And you may wait and I may come?

'I saw the Sibyl at Cumae'

*And the Sibyl, you know. I saw her with my own eyes at Cumae,
hanging in a jar; and, when the boys asked her, 'What would you,
Sibyl?' she answered, 'I would die.'* – PETRONIUS

"I saw the Sibyl at Cumae"
  (One said) "with mine own eye.
She hung in a cage, and read her rune
  To all the passers-by.
Said the boys, 'What wouldst thou, Sibyl?'
  She answered, 'I would die.'"

The Orchard-Pit

a fragment

Piled deep below the screening apple-branch
   They lie with bitter[1] apples in their hands:
And some are only ancient bones that blanch,
And some had ships that last year's wind did launch,
   And some were yesterday the lords of lands.

In the soft dell, among the apple-trees,
   High up above the hidden pit she stands,
And there for ever sings, who gave to these,
That lie below, her magic hour of ease,
   And those her apples holden in their hands.

This in my dreams is shown me; and her hair
   Crosses my lips and draws my burning breath;
Her song spreads golden wings upon the air,
Life's eyes are gleaming from her forehead fair,
   And from her breasts the ravishing eyes of Death.

Men say to me that sleep hath many dreams,
   Yet I knew never but this dream alone:
There, from a dried-up channel, once the stream's,
The glen slopes up; even such in sleep it seems
   As to my waking sight the place well known.

*

My love I call her, and she loves me well:
   But I love her as in the maelstrom's cup
The whirled stone loves the leaf inseparable
That clings to it round all the circling swell,
   And that the same last eddy swallows up.

---

[1] This may be a misprint for 'bitten'. [Ed.]

from

Dante and His Circle:
with the Italian Poets preceding him
(1100-1200-1300)

A Collection of Lyrics
translated in the original metres

Saint Francis of Assisi

CANTICA

Our Lord Christ: of Order[1]

Set Love in order, thou that lovest Me.
  Never was virtue out of order found;
And though I fill thy heart desirously,
  By thine own virtue I must keep My ground:
When to My love thou dost bring charity,
  Even she must come with order girt and gown'd.
    Look how the trees are bound
    To order, bearing fruit;
    And by one thing compute,
In all things earthly, order's grace or gain.

[1] This speech occurs in a long poem on Divine Love, half ecstatic, half scholastic, and hardly appreciable now. The passage stands well by itself, and is the only one spoken by our Lord.

All earthly things I had the making of
    Were numbered and were measured then by Me;
And each was ordered to its end by Love,
    Each kept, through order, clean for ministry.
Charity most of all, when known enough,
    Is of her very nature orderly.
          Lo, now! what heat in thee,
          Soul, can have bred this rout?
          Thou putt'st all order out.
Even this love's heat must be its curb and rein.

Emperor Frederick II

CANZONE

Of his Lady in bondage

For grief I am about to sing,
    Even as another would for joy;
    Mine eyes which the hot tears destroy
Are scarce enough for sorrowing:
To speak of such a grievous thing
    Also my tongue I must employ,
Saying: Woe 's me, who am full of woes!
    Not while I live shall my sighs cease
    For her in whom my heart found peace:
I am become like unto those
    That cannot sleep for weariness,
Now I have lost my crimson rose.

And yet I will not call her lost;
    She is not gone out of the earth;
    She is but girded with a girth
Of hate, that clips her in like frost.

Thus says she every hour almost: –
   "When I was born, 'twas an ill birth!
O that I never had been born.
   If I am still to fall asleep
   Weeping, and when I wake to weep;
If he whom I most loathe and scorn
   Is still to have me his, and keep
Smiling about me night and morn!

"O that I never had been born
   A woman! a poor, helpless fool,
   Who can but stoop beneath the rule
Of him she needs must loathe and scorn!
If ever I feel less forlorn,
   I stand all day in fear and dule,
Lest he discern it, and with rough
   Speech mock at me, or with his smile
   So hard you scarce could call it guile:
No man is there to say, 'Enough.'
   O, but if God waits a long while,
Death cannot always stand aloof!

"Thou, God the Lord, dost know all this:
   Give me a little comfort then,
   Him who is worst among bad men
Smite thou for me. Those limbs of his
Once hidden where the sharp worm is,
   Perhaps I might see hope again.
Yet for a certain period
   Would I seem like as one that saith
   Strange things for grief, and murmureth
With smitten palms and hair abroad:
   Still whispering under my held breath,
'Shall I not praise Thy name, O God?'

"Thou, God the Lord, dost know all this:
   It is a very weary thing
   Thus to be always trembling:

And till the breath of his life cease,
The hate in him will but increase,
    And with his hate my suffering.
Each morn I hear his voice bid them
    That watch me, to be faithful spies
    Lest I go forth and see the skies;
Each night, to each, he saith the same: –
    And in my soul and in mine eyes
There is a burning heat like flame."

Thus grieves she now; but she shall wear
    This love of mine, whereof I spoke,
    About her body for a cloak,
And for a garland in her hair,
Even yet: because I mean to prove,
Not to speak only, this my love.

Guido Guinicelli

SONNET

Concerning Lucy

When Lucy draws her mantle round her face,
    So sweeter than all else she is to see,
    That hence unto the hills there lives not he
Whose whole soul would not love her for her grace.
Then seems she like a daughter of some race
    That holds high rule in France or Germany:
    And a snake's head stricken off suddenly
Throbs never as then throbs my heart to embrace
Her body in these arms, even were she loth; –
    To kiss her lips, to kiss her cheeks, to kiss
        The lids of her two eyes which are two flames.
        Yet what my heart so longs for, my heart blames:
    For surely sorrow might be bred from this
Where some man's patient love abides its growth.

SONNET

He will praise his Lady

Yea, let me praise my lady whom I love:
  Likening her unto the lily and rose:
  Brighter than morning star her visage glows;
She is beneath even as her Saint above;
She is as the air in summer which God wove
  Of purple and of vermilion glorious;
  As gold and jewels richer than man knows.
Love's self, being love for her, must holier prove.
Ever as she walks she hath a sober grace,
  Making bold men abashed and good men glad;
  If she delight thee not, thy heart must err.
No man dare look on her, his thoughts being base:
  Nay, let me say even more than I have said; –
  No man could think base thoughts who looked on her.

CANZONE

Of the Gentle Heart

Within the gentle heart Love shelters him
  As birds within the green shade of the grove.
Before the gentle heart, in nature's scheme,
  Love was not, nor the gentle heart ere Love.
    For with the sun, at once,
So sprang the light immediately; nor was
    Its birth before the sun's.
And Love hath his effect in gentleness
    Of very self; even as
Within the middle fire the heat's excess.

The fire of Love comes to the gentle heart
   Like as its virtue to a precious stone;
To which no star its influence can impart
   Till it is made a pure thing by the sun:
      For when the sun hath smit
From out its essence that which there was vile,
      The star endoweth it.
And so the heart created by God's breath
      Pure, true, and clean from guile,
A woman, like a star, enamoureth.

In gentle heart Love for like reason is
   For which the lamp's high flame is fanned and bow'd:
Clear, piercing bright, it shines for its own bliss;
   Nor would it burn there else, it is so proud.
      For evil natures meet
With Love as it were water met with flame,
      As cold abhorring heat.
Through gentle heart Love doth a track divine, –
      Like knowing like; the same
As diamond runs through iron in the mine.

The sun strikes full upon the mud all day:
   It remains vile, nor the sun's worth is less.
"By race I am gentle," the proud man doth say:
   He is the mud, the sun is gentleness.
      Let no man predicate
That aught the name of gentleness should have,
      Even in a king's estate,
Except the heart there be a gentle man's.
      The star-beam lights the wave, –
Heaven holds the star and the star's radiance.

God, in the understanding of high Heaven,
   Burns more than in our sight the living sun:
There to behold His Face unveiled is given;
   And Heaven, whose will is homage paid to One
      Fulfils the things which live

In God, from the beginning excellent.
　　So should my lady give
That truth which in her eyes is glorified,
　　On which her heart is bent,
To me whose service waiteth at her side.

My lady, God shall ask, "What daredst thou?"
　　(When my soul stands with all her acts review'd;)
"Thou passedst Heaven, into My sight, as now,
　　To make Me of vain love similitude.
　　　　To Me doth praise belong,
And to the Queen of all the realm of grace
　　Who slayeth fraud and wrong."
Then may I plead: "As though from Thee he came,
　　Love wore an angel's face:
Lord, if I loved her, count it not my shame."

Giacomino Pugliesi, Knight of Prato

CANZONE

Of his Dead Lady

Death, why hast thou made life so hard to bear,
　　Taking my lady hence? Hast thou no whit
Of shame? The youngest flower and the most fair
　　Thou hast plucked away, and the world wanteth it.
O leaden Death, hast thou no pitying?
Our warm love's very spring
　　Thou stopp'st, and endest what was holy and meet;
And of my gladdening
Mak'st a most woful thing,
And in my heart dost bid the bird not sing
　　That sang so sweet.

Once the great joy and solace that I had
    Was more than is with other gentlemen: –
Now is my love gone hence, who made me glad.
    With her that hope I lived in she hath ta'en
And left me nothing but these sighs and tears, –
Nothing of the old years
    That come not back again,
Wherein I was so happy, being hers.
Now to mine eyes her face no more appears,
Nor doth her voice make music in mine ears,
    As it did then.

O God, why hast thou made my grief so deep?
    Why set me in the dark to grope and pine?
Why parted me from her companionship,
    And crushed the hope which was a gift of thine?
To think, dear, that I never any more
Can see thee as before!
    Who is it shuts thee in?
Who hides that smile for which my heart is sore,
And drowns those words that I am longing for,
    Lady of mine?

Where is my lady, and the lovely face
    She had, and the sweet motion when she walk'd? –
Her chaste, mild favour – her so delicate grace –
    Her eyes, her mouth, and the dear way she talk'd? –
Her courteous bending – her most noble air –
The soft fall of her hair? . . .
My lady – she to whom my soul
    A gladness brought!
Now I do never see her anywhere,
And may not, looking in her eyes, gain there
    The blessing which I sought.

So if I had the realm of Hungary,
    With Greece, and all the Almayn even to France,
Or Saint Sophia's treasure-hoard, you see

All could not give me back her countenance.
For since the day when my dear lady died
From us, (with God being born and glorified,)
   No more pleasaunce
Her image bringeth, seated at my side,
But only tears. Ay me! the strength and pride
   Which it brought once.

Had I my will, beloved, I would say
   To God, unto whose bidding all things bow,
That we were still together night and day:
   Yet be it done as His behests allow.
I do remember that while she remain'd
With me, she often called me her sweet friend;
   But does not now,
Because God drew her towards Him, in the end.
Lady, that peace which none but He can send
   Be thine. Even so.

Ubaldo di Marco

SONNET

Of a Lady's Love for him

My body resting in a haunt of mine,
   I ranged among alternate memories;
   What while an unseen noble lady's eyes
Were fixed upon me, yet she gave no sign;
To stay and go she sweetly did incline,
   Always afraid lest there were any spies;
   Then reached to me, – and smelt it in sweet wise,
And reached to me – some sprig of bloom or bine.

Conscious of perfume, on my side I leant,
  And rose upon my feet, and gazed around
    To see the plant whose flower could so beguile.
Finding it not, I sought it by the scent;
  And by the scent, in truth, the plant I found,
    And rested in its shadow a great while.

Folgore da San Geminiano

OF THE MONTHS

TWELVE SONNETS

Addressed to a Fellowship of Sienese Nobles

DEDICATION

Unto the blithe and lordly Fellowship,
  (I know not where, but wheresoe'er, I know,
  Lordly and blithe,) be greeting; and thereto,
Dogs, hawks, and a full purse wherein to dip;
Quails struck i' the flight; nags mettled to the whip;
  Hart-hounds, hare-hounds, and blood-hounds even so;
  And o'er that realm, a crown for Niccolò,
Whose praise in Siena springs from lip to lip.
Tingoccio, Atuin di Togno, and Ancaiàn,
  Bartolo and Mugaro and Faënot,
Who well might pass for children of King Ban,
  Courteous and valiant more than Lancelot, –
To each, God speed! how worthy every man
  To hold high tournament in Camelot.

JANUARY

For January I give you vests of skins,
  And mighty fires in hall, and torches lit;
  Chambers and happy beds with all things fit;
Smooth silken sheets, rough furry counterpanes;
And sweetmeats baked; and one that deftly spins
  Warm arras; and Douay cloth, and store of it;
  And on this merry manner still to twit
The wind, when most his mastery the wind wins.
Or issuing forth at seasons in the day,
  Ye'll fling soft handfuls of the fair white snow
Among the damsels standing round, in play:
  And when you all are tired and all aglow,
Indoors again the court shall hold its sway,
  And the free Fellowship continue so.

FEBRUARY

In February I give you gallant sport
  Of harts and hinds and great wild boars; and all
  Your company good foresters and tall,
With buskins strong, with jerkins close and short;
And in your leashes, hounds of brave report;
  And from your purses, plenteous money-fall,
  In very spleen of misers' starveling gall,
Who at your generous customs snarl and snort.
At dusk wend homeward, ye and all your folk,
  All laden from the wilds, to your carouse,
    With merriment and songs accompanied:
And so draw wine and let the kitchen smoke;
  And so be till the first watch glorious;
    Then sound sleep to you till the day be wide.

MARCH

In March I give you plenteous fisheries
    Of lamprey and of salmon, eel and trout,
    Dental and dolphin, sturgeon, all the rout
Of fish in all the streams that fill the seas.
With fishermen and fishing-boats at ease,
    Sail-barques and arrow-barques, and galleons stout,
    To bear you, while the season lasts, far out,
And back, through spring, to any port you please.
But with fair mansions see that it be fill'd,
    With everything exactly to your mind,
      And every sort of comfortable folk.
No convent suffer there, nor priestly guild:
    Leave the mad monks to preach after their kind
      Their scanty truth, their lies beyond a joke.

APRIL

I give you meadow-lands in April, fair
    With over-growth of beautiful green grass;
    There among fountains the glad hours shall pass,
And pleasant ladies bring you solace there.
With steeds of Spain and ambling palfreys rare;
    Provençal songs and dances that surpass;
    And quaint French mummings; and through hollow brass
A sound of German music on the air.
And gardens ye shall have, that every one
    May lie at ease about the fragrant place;
      And each with fitting reverence shall bow down
      Unto that youth to whom I gave a crown
    Of precious jewels like to those that grace
The Babylonian Kaiser, Prester John.

MAY

I give you horses for your games in May,
  And all of them well trained unto the course, –
  Each docile, swift, erect, a goodly horse;
With armour on their chests, and bells at play
Between their brows, and pennons fair and gay;
  Fine nets, and housings meet for warriors,
  Emblazoned with the shields ye claim for yours;
Gules, argent, or, all dizzy at noonday.
And spears shall split, and fruit go flying up
In merry counterchange for wreaths that drop
  From balconies and casements far above;
And tender damsels with young men and youths
Shall kiss together on the cheeks and mouths;
  And every day be glad with joyful love.

JUNE

In June I give you a close-wooded fell,
  With crowns of thicket coiled about its head,
  With thirty villas twelve times turreted,
All girdling round a little citadel;
And in the midst a springhead and fair well
  With thousand conduits branched and shining speed,
  Wounding the garden and the tender mead,
Yet to the freshened grass acceptable.
And lemons, citrons, dates, and oranges,
  And all the fruits whose savour is most rare,
Shall shine within the shadow of your trees;
  And every one shall be a lover there;
Until your life, so filled with courtesies,
  Throughout the world be counted debonair.

For July, in Siena, by the willow-tree,
   I give you barrels of white Tuscan wine
   In ice far down your cellars stored supine;
And morn and eve to eat in company
Of those vast jellies dear to you and me;
   Of partridges and youngling pheasants sweet,
   Boiled capons, sovereign kids: and let their treat
Be veal and garlic, with whom these agree.
Let time slip by, till by-and-by, all day;
   And never swelter through the heat at all,
But move at ease at home, sound, cool, and gay;
   And wear sweet-coloured robes that lightly fall;
And keep your tables set in fresh array,
   Not coaxing spleen to be your seneschal.

For August, be your dwelling thirty towers
   Within an Alpine valley mountainous,
   Where never the sea-wind may vex your house,
But clear life separate, like a star, be yours.
There horses shall wait saddled at all hours,
   That ye may mount at morning or at eve:
   On each hand either ridge ye shall perceive,
A mile apart, which soon a good beast scours.
So alway, drawing homewards, ye shall tread
   Your valley parted by a rivulet
     Which day and night shall flow sedate and smooth.
There all through noon ye may possess the shade,
   And there your open purses shall entreat
     The best of Tuscan cheer to feed your youth.

And in September, O what keen delight!
   Falcons and astors, merlins, sparrowhawks;
   Decoy-birds that shall lure your game in flocks;
And hounds with bells: and gauntlets stout and tight;
Wide pouches; crossbows shooting out of sight;
   Arblasts and javelins; balls and ball-cases;
   All birds the best to fly at; moulting these,
Those reared by hand; with finches mean and slight;
And for their chase, all birds the best to fly;
   And each to each of you be lavish still
     In gifts; and robbery find no gainsaying;
And if you meet with travellers going by,
   Their purses from your purse's flow shall fill;
     And avarice be the only outcast thing.

OCTOBER

Next, for October, to some sheltered coign
   Flouting the winds, I'll hope to find you slunk;
   Though in bird-shooting (lest all sport be sunk),
Your foot still press the turf, the horse your groin.
At night with sweethearts in the dance you'll join,
   And drink the blessed must, and get quite drunk,
   There's no such life for any human trunk;
And that's a truth that rings like golden coin!
Then, out of bed again when morning 's come,
   Let your hands drench your face refreshingly,
     And take your physic roast, with flask and knife.
Sounder and snugger you shall feel at home
   Than lake-fish, river-fish, or fish at sea,
     Inheriting the cream of Christian life.

NOVEMBER

Let baths and wine-butts be November's due,
  With thirty mule-loads of broad gold-pieces;
  And canopy with silk the streets that freeze;
And keep your drink-horns steadily in view.
Let every trader have his gain of you:
  Clareta shall your lamps and torches send, –
  Caëta, citron-candies without end;
And each shall drink, and help his neighbour to.
And let the cold be great, and the fire grand:
  And still for fowls, and pastries sweetly wrought,
    For hares and kids, for roast and boiled, be sure
You always have your appetites at hand;
  And then let night howl and heaven fall, so nought
    Be missed that makes a man's bed-furniture.

DECEMBER

Last, for December, houses on the plain,
  Ground-floors to live on, logs heaped mountain-high,
  And carpets stretched, and newest games to try,
And torches lit, and gifts from man to man:
(Your host, a drunkard and a Catalan;)
  And whole dead pigs, and cunning cooks to ply
  Each throat with tit-bits that shall satisfy;
And wine-butts of Saint Galganus' brave span.
And be your coats well-lined and tightly bound,
  And wrap yourselves in cloaks of strength and weight,
    With gallant hoods to put your faces through.
And make your game of abject vagabond
  Abandoned miserable reprobate
    Misers; don't let them have a chance with you.

And now take thought, my sonnet, who is he
  That most is full of every gentleness;
  And say to him (for thou shalt quickly guess
His name) that all his 'hests are law to me.
For if I held fair Paris town in fee,
  And were not called his friend, 'twere surely less.
  Ah! had he but the emperor's wealth, my place
Were fitted in his love more steadily
Than is Saint Francis at Assisi. Alway
  Commend him unto me and his, – not least
    To Caian, held so dear in the blithe band.
"Folgore da San Geminiano" (say),
  "Has sent me, charging me to travel fast,
    Because his heart went with you in your hand."

Pier Moronelli, di Fiorenza

CANZONETTA

A Bitter Song to his Lady

O lady amorous,
Merciless lady,
Full blithely play'd ye
These your beguilings.
So with an urchin
A man makes merry, –
In mirth grows clamorous,
Laughs and rejoices, –
But when his choice is
To fall aweary,
Cheats him with silence.
This is Love's portion: –

In much wayfaring
With many burdens
He loads his servants,
But at the sharing,
The underservice
And overservice
Are alike barren.

As my disaster
Your jest I cherish,
And well may perish.
Even so a falcon
Is sometimes taken
And scantily cautell'd;
Till when his master
At length to loose him,
To train and use him,
Is after all gone, –
The creature's throttled
And will not waken.
Wherefore, my lady,
If you will own me,
O look upon me!
If I'm not thought on,
At least perceive me!
O do not leave me
So much forgotten!

If, lady, truly
You wish my profit,
What follows of it
Though still you say so? –
For all your well-wishes
I still am waiting.
I grow unruly,
And deem at last I'm
Only your pastime.
A child will play so,

Who greatly relishes
Sporting and petting
With a little wild bird:
Unaware he kills it, –
Then turns it, feels it,
Calls it with a mild word,
Is angry after, –
Then again in laughter
Loud is the child heard.

O my delightful
My own my lady,
Upon the Mayday
Which brought me to you
Was all my haste then
But a fool's venture?
To have my sight full
Of you propitious
Truly my wish was,
And to pursue you
And let love chasten
My heart to the centre.
But warming, lady,
May end in burning.
Of all this yearning
What comes, I beg you?
In all your glances
What is't a man sees? –
Fever and ague.

Niccolò degli Albizzi

PROLONGED SONNET

When the Troops were returning from Milan

If you could see, fair brother, how dead beat
   The fellows look who come through Rome to-day, –
   Black yellow smoke-dried visages, – you'd say
They thought their haste at going all too fleet.
Their empty victual-waggons up the street
   Over the bridge dreadfully sound and sway;
   Their eyes, as hanged men's, turning the wrong way;
And nothing on their backs, or heads, or feet.
One sees the ribs and all the skeletons
   Of their gaunt horses; and a sorry sight
Are the torn saddles, crammed with straw and stones.
   They are ashamed, and march throughout the night;
Stumbling, for hunger, on their marrowbones;
   Like barrels rolling, jolting, in this plight.
Their arms all gone, not even their swords are saved;
And each as silent as a man being shaved.

Dante Alighieri

from
The New Life

[Dante invites his fellow poets to interpret his dream of Beatrice.]

To every heart which the sweet pain doth move,
   And unto which these words may now be brought
   For true interpretation and kind thought,
Be greeting in our Lord's name, which is Love.

Of those long hours wherein the stars, above,
   Wake and keep watch, the third was almost nought,
   When Love was shown me with such terrors fraught
As may not carelessly be spoken of.
He seemed like one who is full of joy, and had
   My heart within his hand, and on his arm
   My lady, with a mantle round her, slept;
Whom (having wakened her) anon he made
   To eat that heart; she ate, as fearing harm.
   Then he went out; and as he went, he wept.

*

[Dante writes a poem, which purports to be a lament for the departure of an
    unnamed lady. In fact it reflects the pain of his love for Beatrice.]

All ye that pass along Love's trodden way,
Pause ye awhile and say
   If there be any grief like unto mine:
I pray you that you hearken a short space
Patiently, if my case
   Be not a piteous marvel and a sign.

Love (never, certes, for my worthless part,
But of his own great heart),
   Vouchsafed to me a life so calm and sweet
That oft I heard folk question as I went
What such great gladness meant: –
   They spoke of it behind me in the street.

But now that fearless bearing is all gone
   Which with Love's hoarded wealth was given me;
   Till I am grown to be
So poor that I have dread to think thereon.

And thus it is that I, being like as one
   Who is ashamed and hides his poverty,
   Without seem full of glee,
And let my heart within travail and moan.

*

[Dante on a journey encounters Love in the guise of a traveller.]

A day agone, as I rode sullenly
   Upon a certain path that liked me not,
   I met Love midway while the air was hot,
Clothed lightly as a wayfarer might be.
And for the cheer he showed, he seemed to me
   As one who hath lost lordship he had got;
   Advancing tow'rds me full of sorrowful thought,
Bowing his forehead so that none should see.
Then as I went, he called me by my name,
   Saying: "I journey since the morn was dim
     Thence where I made thy heart to be: which now
I needs must bear unto another dame."
   Wherewith so much passed into me of him
     That he was gone, and I discerned not how.

*

[He resolves to write only in praise of Beatrice and addresses his poem to other
ladies of comparable refinement and understanding.]

Ladies that have intelligence in love,
   Of mine own lady I would speak with you;
   Not that I hope to count her praises through,
     But telling what I may, to ease my mind.
And I declare that when I speak thereof,
Love sheds such perfect sweetness over me

That if my courage failed not, certainly
    To him my listeners must be all resign'd.
    Wherefore I will not speak in such large kind
That mine own speech should foil me, which were base;
But only will discourse of her high grace
    In these poor words, the best that I can find,
With you alone, dear dames and damozels:
'Twere ill to speak thereof with any else.

An Angel of his blessed knowledge, saith
    To God: "Lord, in the world that Thou hast made,
    A miracle in action is display'd,
    By reason of a soul whose splendours fare
Even hither: and since Heaven requireth
    Nought saving her, for her it prayeth Thee,
    Thy Saints crying aloud continually."
    Yet Pity still defends our earthly share
    In that sweet soul; God answering thus the prayer:
"My well-belovèd, suffer that in peace
Your hope remain, while so My pleasure is,
    There where one dwells who dreads the loss of her:
And who in Hell unto the doomed shall say,
'I have looked on that for which God's chosen pray.'"

My lady is desired in the high Heaven:
    Wherefore, it now behoveth me to tell,
    Saying: Let any maid that would be well
    Esteemed keep with her: for as she goes by,
Into foul hearts a deathly chill is driven
By Love, that makes ill thought to perish there:
While any who endures to gaze on her
    Must either be ennobled, or else die.
    When one deserving to be raised so high
Is found, 'tis then her power attains its proof,
Making his heart strong for his soul's behoof
    With the full strength of meek humility.
Also this virtue owns she, by God's will:
Who speaks with her can never come to ill.

Love saith concerning her: "How chanceth it
  That flesh, which is of dust, should be thus pure?"
    Then, gazing always, he makes oath: "Forsure,
      This is a creature of God till now unknown."
She hath that paleness of the pearl that 's fit
In a fair woman, so much and not more;
She is as high as Nature's skill can soar;
    Beauty is tried by her comparison.
      Whatever her sweet eyes are turned upon,
Spirits of love do issue thence in flame,
Which through their eyes who then may look on them
    Pierce to the heart's deep chamber every one.
And in her smile Love's image you may see;
Whence none can gaze upon her steadfastly.

Dear Song, I know thou wilt hold gentle speech
  With many ladies, when I send thee forth:
    Wherefore (being mindful that thou hadst thy birth
      From Love, and art a modest, simple child,)
Whomso thou meetest, say thou this to each:
"Give me good speed! To her I wend along
In whose much strength my weakness is made strong."
    And if, i' the end, thou wouldst not be beguiled
      Of all thy labour seek not the defiled
And common sort; but rather choose to be
Where man and woman dwell in courtesy.
    So to the road thou shalt be reconciled,
And find the lady, and with the lady, Love.
Commend thou me to each, as doth behove.

                    *

[In response to a friend's question, he discourses on the nature of love.]

  Love and the gentle heart are one same thing,
    Even as the wise man* in his ditty saith:
      Each, of itself, would be such life in death
    As rational soul bereft of reasoning.

'Tis Nature makes them when she loves: a king
 Love is, whose palace where he sojourneth
 Is called the Heart; there draws he quiet breath
At first, with brief or longer slumbering.
Then beauty seen in virtuous womankind
 Will make the eyes desire, and through the heart
 Send the desiring of the eyes again;
Where often it abides so long enshrin'd
 That Love at length out of his sleep will start.
 And women feel the same for worthy men.

* Guido Guinicelli, in the canzone which begins, 'Within the gentle heart Love shelters him'. (See above, page 104.)

*

[He meets Beatrice in the street, walking behind Giovanna, the Lady loved by his friend Cavalcanti.]

I felt a spirit of love begin to stir
 Within my heart, long time unfelt till then;
 And saw Love coming towards me fair and fain,
(That I scarce knew him for his joyful cheer),
Saying, "Be now indeed my worshipper!"
 And in his speech he laugh'd and laugh'd again.
 Then, while it was his pleasure to remain,
I chanced to look the way he had drawn near,
And saw the Ladies Joan and Beatrice
 Approach me, this the other following,
 One and a second marvel instantly.
And even as now my memory speaketh this,
 Love spake it then: "The first is christen'd Spring;*
 The second Love, she is so like to me."

* In his commentary, Dante plays on the words *Primavera* (Spring) and *prima verrà* (she shall come first). He then draws a near-blasphemous analogy between the Joan (or Giovanna) who comes first in the poem and "that John [or Giovanni] who went before the True Light", preparing the way of the Lord. [Ed.]

*

[He has a premonition of Beatrice's death.]

A very pitiful lady, very young,
  Exceeding rich in human sympathies,
    Stood by, what time I clamour'd upon Death
And at the wild words wandering on my tongue
  And at the piteous look within mine eyes
    She was affrighted, that sobs choked her breath.
    So by her weeping where I lay beneath,
Some other gentle ladies came to know
My state, and made her go:
Afterward, bending themselves over me,
One said, 'Awaken thee!'
    And one, 'What thing thy sleep disquieteth?'
With that, my soul woke up from its eclipse,
The while my lady's name rose to my lips:

But utter'd in a voice so sob-broken,
  So feeble with the agony of tears,
    That I alone might hear it in my heart;
And though that look was on my visage then
  Which he who is ashamed so plainly wears,
    Love made that I through shame held not apart,
    But gazed upon them. And my hue was such
That they look'd at each other and thought of death;
Saying under their breath
Most tenderly, 'O let us comfort him:'
Then unto me: 'What dream
    Was thine, that it hath shaken thee so much?'
And when I was a little comforted,
'This, ladies, was the dream I dreamt,' I said.

"I was a-thinking how life fails with us
  Suddenly after such a little while;
    When Love sobb'd in my heart, which is his home.

125

Whereby my spirit wax'd so dolorous
    That in myself I said, with sick recoil:
        'Yea, to my lady too this Death must come.'
        And therewithal such a bewilderment
Possess'd me, that I shut mine eyes for peace;
And in my brain did cease
Order of thought, and every healthful thing.
Afterwards, wandering
        Amid a swarm of doubts that came and went,
Some certain women's faces hurried by,
And shrieked to me, 'Thou too shalt die, shalt die!'

"Then saw I many broken hinted sights
    In the uncertain state I stepp'd into.
        Meseem'd to be I know not in what place,
Where ladies through the streets, like mournful lights,
    Ran with loose hair, and eyes that frighten'd you,
        By their own terror, and a pale amaze:
        The while, little by little, as I thought,
The sun ceased, and the stars began to gather,
And each wept at the other;
And birds dropp'd in mid-flight out of the sky;
And earth shook suddenly;
        And I was 'ware of one, hoarse and tired out,
Who ask'd of me: 'Hast thou not heard it said?...
Thy lady, she that was so fair, is dead.'

"Then lifting up mine eyes, as the tears came,
    I saw the Angels, like a rain of manna,
        In a long flight flying back Heavenward;
Having a little cloud in front of them,
    After the which they went and said, 'Hosanna';
        And if they had said more, you should have heard.
        Then Love said, 'Now shall all things be made clear:
Come and behold our lady where she lies.'
These 'wildering phantasies
Then carried me to see my lady dead.
Even as I there was led,

Her ladies with a veil were covering her;
And with her was such very humbleness
That she appeared to say, 'I am at peace.'

"And I became so humble in my grief,
   Seeing in her such deep humility,
      That I said: 'Death, I hold thee passing good
Henceforth, and a most gentle sweet relief,
   Since my dear love has chosen to dwell with thee:
      Pity, not hate, is thine, well understood.
      Lo! I do so desire to see thy face
That I am like as one who nears the tomb;
My soul entreats thee, Come.'
Then I departed, having made my moan;
And when I was alone
      I said, and cast my eyes to the High Place:
'Blessed is he, fair soul, who meets thy glance!'
...Just then you woke me, of your complaisaùnce."

*

[He writes a poem for a friend in memory of a Lady who has died. In the first
   stanza, the friend laments; in the second, Dante speaks in his own person.]

Whatever while the thought comes over me
   That I may not again
      Behold that lady whom I mourn for now,
About my heart my mind brings constantly
   So much of extreme pain
      That I say, Soul of mine, why stayest thou?
      Truly the anguish, soul, that we must bow
Beneath, until we win out of this life,
   Gives me full oft a fear that trembleth:
   So that I call on Death
Even as on Sleep one calleth after strife,
Saying, Come unto me. Life showeth grim
And bare; and if one dies, I envy him.

127

For ever, among all my sighs which burn,
   There is a piteous speech
     That clamours upon death continually:
Yea, unto him doth my whole spirit turn
   Since first his hand did reach
     My lady's life with most foul cruelty.
     But from the height of woman's fairness, she,
Going up from us with the joy we had,
   Grew perfectly and spiritually fair;
   That so she spreads even there
A light of Love which makes the Angels glad,
And even unto their subtle minds can bring
A certain awe of profound marvelling.

*

[A woman at her window, observing Dante's grief after the death of Beatrice,
pities him and inspires a kind of love in him.]

A gentle thought there is will often start,
   Within my secret self, to speech of thee:
   Also of Love it speaks so tenderly
That much in me consents and takes its part.
"And what is this," the soul saith to the heart,
   "That cometh thus to comfort thee and me,
   And thence where it would dwell, thus potently
Can drive all other thoughts by its strange art?"
And the heart answers: "Be no more at strife
   'Twixt doubt and doubt: this is Love's messenger
     And speaketh but his words, from him received;
And all the strength it owns and all the life
   It draweth from the gentle eyes of her
     Who, looking on our grief, hath often grieved."

*

128

[He addresses a company of pilgrims passing through Florence.]

Ye pilgrim-folk, advancing pensively
    As if in thought of distant things, I pray,
    Is your own land indeed so far away –
As by your aspect it would seem to be –
That this our heavy sorrow leaves you free
    Though passing through the mournful town mid-way;
    Like unto men that understand to-day
Nothing at all of her great misery?
Yet if ye will but stay, whom I accost,
    And listen to my words a little space,
        At going ye shall mourn with a loud voice.
It is her Beatrice that she hath lost;
    Of whom the least word spoken holds such grace
        That men weep hearing it, and have no choice.

*

[In the final sonnet, he prefigures *The Divine Comedy*.]

Beyond the sphere which spreads to widest space
    Now soars the sigh that my heart sends above;
    A new perception born of grieving Love
Guideth it upward the untrodden ways.
When it hath reached unto the end, and stays,
    It sees a lady round whom splendours move
    In homage; till, by the great light thereof
Abashed, the pilgrim spirit stands at gaze.
It sees her such, that when it tells me this
    Which it hath seen, I understand it not,
        It hath a speech so subtile and so fine.
    And yet I know its voice within my thought
Often remembereth me of Beatrice:
        So that I understand it, ladies mine.

129

SESTINA[1]

Of the Lady Pietra degli Scrovigni

To the dim light and the large circle of shade
I have clomb, and to the whitening of the hills,
There where we see no colour in the grass.
Natheless my longing loses not its green,
It has so taken root in the hard stone
Which talks and hears as though it were a lady.

Utterly frozen is this youthful lady,
Even as the snow that lies within the shade;
For she is no more moved than is the stone
By the sweet season which makes warm the hills
And alters them afresh from white to green,
Covering their sides again with flowers and grass.

When on her hair she sets a crown of grass
The thought has no more room for other lady,
Because she weaves the yellow with the green
So well that Love sits down there in the shade, –
Love who has shut me in among low hills
Faster than between walls of granite-stone.

She is more bright than is a precious stone;
The wound she gives may not be healed with grass:
I therefore have fled far o'er plains and hills
For refuge from so dangerous a lady;
But from her sunshine nothing can give shade, –
Not any hill, nor wall, nor summer-green.

[1] I have translated this piece both on account of its great and peculiar beauty, and also because it affords an example of a form of composition which I have met with in no Italian writer before Dante's time, though it is not uncommon among the Provençal poets (see Dante, *De Vulg. Eloq.*). I have headed it with the name of a Paduan lady, to whom it is surmised by some to have been addressed during Dante's exile; but this must be looked upon as a rather doubtful conjecture and I have adopted the name chiefly to mark it at once as not referring to Beatrice.

A while ago, I saw her dressed in green, –
So fair, she might have wakened in a stone
This love which I do feel even for her shade;
And therefore, as one woos a graceful lady,
I wooed her in a field that was all grass
Girdled about with very lofty hills.

Yet shall the streams turn back and climb the hills
Before Love's flame in this damp wood and green
Burn, as it burns within a youthful lady,
For my sake, who would sleep away in stone
My life, or feed like beasts upon the grass,
Only to see her garments cast a shade.

How dark soe'er the hills throw out their shade,
Under her summer-green the beautiful lady
Covers it, like a stone cover'd in grass.

Guido Cavalcanti

SONNET

To Dante Alighieri

He interprets Dante's Dream, related to the first Sonnet of the Vita Nuova[1]

Unto my thinking, thou beheld'st all worth,
    All joy, as much of good as man may know,
    If thou wert in his power who here below
Is honour's righteous lord throughout this earth.
Where evil dies, even there he has his birth,
    Whose justice out of pity's self doth grow.
    Softly to sleeping persons he will go,
And, with no pain to them, their hearts draw forth.

[1] See *The New Life*, p.119 above.

Thy heart he took, as knowing well, alas!
  That Death had claimed thy lady for a prey:
    In fear whereof, he fed her with thy heart.
    But when he seemed in sorrow to depart,
  Sweet was thy dream; for by that sign, I say,
Surely the opposite shall come to pass.[1]

[1] This may refer to the belief that, towards morning, dreams go by contraries.

SONNET

He compares all Things with his Lady, and finds them wanting

Beauty in woman; the high will's decree;
  Fair knighthood armed for manly exercise;
  The pleasant song of birds; love's soft replies;
The strength of rapid ships upon the sea;
The serene air when light begins to be;
  The white snow, without wind that falls and lies;
  Fields of all flower; the place where waters rise;
Silver and gold; azure in jewellery: –
Weighed against these, the sweet and quiet worth
  Which my dear lady cherishes at heart
    Might seem a little matter to be shown;
  Being truly, over these, as much apart
As the whole heaven is greater than this earth.
    All good to kindred natures cleaveth soon.

SONNET

A Rapture concerning his Lady

Who is she coming, whom all gaze upon,
   Who makes the air all tremulous with light,
And at whose side is Love himself? that none
   Dare speak, but each man's sighs are infinite.
   Ah me! how she looks round from left to right,
Let Love discourse: I may not speak thereon.
Lady she seems of such high benison
   As makes all others graceless in men's sight.
The honour which is hers cannot be said;
   To whom are subject all things virtuous,
    While all things beauteous own her deity.
Ne'er was the mind of man so nobly led,
   Nor yet was such redemption granted us
    That we should ever know her perfectly.

BALLATA

Of his Lady among other Ladies

With other women I beheld my love; –
   Not that the rest were women to mine eyes,
Who only as her shadows seemed to move.

I do not praise her more than with the truth,
   Nor blame I these if it be rightly read.

But while I speak, a thought I may not soothe
   Says to my senses: "Soon shall ye be dead,
   If for my sake your tears ye will not shed."

And then the eyes yield passage, at that thought,
To the heart's weeping, which forgets her not.

133

To Guido Orlandi

Of a consecrated Image resembling his Lady

Guido, an image of my lady dwells
  At San Michele in Orto, consecrate
  And duly worshipped. Fair in holy state
She listens to the tale each sinner tells:
And among them that come to her, who ails
  The most, on him the most doth blessing wait.
  She bids the fiend men's bodies abdicate;
Over the curse of blindness she prevails,
And heals sick languors in the public squares.
  A multitude adores her reverently:
    Before her face two burning tapers are;
    Her voice is uttered upon paths afar.
  Yet through the Lesser Brethren's[1] jealousy
She is named idol; not being one of theirs.

---

[1] The Franciscans, in profession of deeper poverty and humility than belonged to other Orders, called themselves *Fratres minores*.

He reveals, in a Dialogue, his increasing Love for Mandetta

Being in thought of love, I chanced to see
  Two youthful damozels.
  One sang: "Our life inhales
  All love continually."

Their aspect was so utterly serene,
  So courteous, of such quiet nobleness,
That I said to them: "Yours, I may well ween,

'Tis of all virtue to unlock the place.
  Ah! damozels, do not account him base
    Whom thus his wound subdues:
    Since I was at Thoulouse,
      My heart is dead in me."

They turned their eyes upon me in so much
  As to perceive how wounded was my heart;
While, of the spirits born of tears, one such
  Had been begotten through the constant smart.
  Then seeing me, abashed, to turn apart,
    One of them said, and laugh'd:
    "Love, look you, by his craft
      Holds this man thoroughly."

But with grave sweetness, after a brief while,
  She who at first had laughed on me replied,
Saying: "This lady, who by Love's great guile
  Her countenance in thy heart has glorified,
  Look'd thee so deep within the eyes, Love sigh'd
    And was awakened there.
    If it seem ill to bear,
      In him thy hope must be."

The second piteous maiden, of all ruth,
  Fashioned for sport in Love's own image, said:
"This stroke, whereof thy heart bears trace in sooth,
  From eyes of too much puïssance was shed,
  Whence in thy heart such brightness enterèd,
    Thou mayst not look thereon.
    Say, of those eyes that shone
      Canst thou remember thee?"

Then said I, yielding answer therewithal
  Unto this virgin's difficult behest:
"A lady of Thoulouse, whom Love doth call
  Mandetta, sweetly kirtled and enlac'd,
  I do remember to my sore unrest.

Yea, by her eyes indeed
My life has been decreed
    To death inevitably."

Go, Ballad, to the city, even Thoulouse,
    And softly entering the Dauràde,[1] look round
    And softly call, that so there may be found
Some lady who for compleasaunce may choose
To show thee her who can my life confuse.
        And if she yield thee way,
        Lift thou thy voice and say:
            "For grace I come to thee."

[1] The ancient church of the Dauràde still exists at Thoulouse. It was so called from the golden effect of the mosaics adorning it.

BALLATA

Of a continual Death in Love

Though thou, indeed, hast quite forgotten ruth,
Its steadfast truth my heart abandons not;
But still its thought yields service in good part
        To that hard heart in thee.

Alas! who hears believes not I am so.
Yet who can know? of very surety, none,
From Love is won a spirit, in some wise,
        Which dies perpetually:

And, when at length in that strange ecstasy
        The heavy sigh will start,
        There rains upon my heart
        A love so pure and fine,
That I say: "Lady, I am wholly thine."[1]

[1] I may take this opportunity of mentioning that, in every case where an abrupt change of metre occurs in one of my translations, it is so also in the original poem.

SONNET

To a Friend who does not pity his Love

If I entreat this lady that all grace
   Seem not unto her heart an enemy,
   Foolish and evil thou declarest me,
And desperate in idle stubbornness.
Whence is such cruel judgment thine, whose face,
   ` To him that looks thereon, professeth thee
   Faithful, and wise, and of all courtesy,
And made after the way of gentleness?
Alas! my soul within my heart doth find
   Sighs, and its grief by weeping doth enhance,
     That, drowned in bitter tears, those sighs depart:
And then there seems a presence in the mind,
   As of a lady's thoughtful countenance
     Come to behold the death of the poor heart.

SONNET

To Dante Alighieri

He rebukes Dante for his way of Life, after the Death of Beatrice[1]

I come to thee by daytime constantly,
   But in thy thoughts too much of baseness find:
   Greatly it grieves me for thy gentle mind,
And for thy many virtues gone from thee.
It was thy wont to shun much company,
   Unto all sorry concourse ill inclin'd:
   And still thy speech of me, heartfelt and kind,
Had made me treasure up thy poetry.

[1] This interesting sonnet must refer to the same period of Dante's
life regarding which he has made Beatrice address him in words of
noble reproach when he meets her in Eden. (*Purgatorio* xxx)

137

But now I dare not, for thine abject life,
    Make manifest that I approve thy rhymes;
        Nor come I in such sort that thou mayst know.
    Ah! prythee read this sonnet many times:
So shall that evil one who bred this strife
    Be thrust from thy dishonoured soul and go.

BALLATA

In Exile at Sarzana

Because I think not ever to return,
    Ballad, to Tuscany, –
    Go therefore thou for me
      Straight to my lady's face,
      Who, of her noble grace,
    Shall show thee courtesy.

Thou seekest her in charge of many sighs,
    Full of much grief and of exceeding fear.
But have good heed thou come not to the eyes
    Of such as are sworn foes to gentle cheer:
    For, certes, if this thing should chance, – from her
        Thou then couldst only look
        For scorn, and such rebuke
        As needs must bring me pain; –
        Yea, after death again
        Tears and fresh agony.

Surely thou knowest, Ballad, how that Death
    Assails me, till my life is almost sped:
Thou knowest how my heart still travaileth
    Through the sore pangs which in my soul are bred: –
    My body being now so nearly dead,

It cannot suffer more.
Then, going, I implore
That this my soul thou take
(Nay, do so for my sake,)
When my heart sets it free.

Ah! Ballad, unto thy dear offices
I do commend my soul, thus trembling;
That thou mayst lead it, for pure piteousness,
Even to that lady's presence whom I sing.
Ah! Ballad, say thou to her, sorrowing,
Whereso thou meet her then: –
"This thy poor handmaiden
Is come, nor will be gone,
Being parted now from one
Who served Love painfully."

Thou also, thou bewildered voice and weak,
That goest forth in tears from my grieved heart,
Shalt, with my soul and with this ballad, speak
Of my dead mind, when thou dost hence depart,
Unto that lady (piteous as thou art!)
Who is so calm and bright,
It shall be deep delight
To feel her presence there.
And thou, Soul, worship her
Still in her purity.

Cino da Pistoia

CANZONE

To Dante Alighieri
On the Death of Beatrice Portinari

Albeit my prayers have not so long delay'd,
   But craved for thee, ere this, that Pity and Love
   Which only bring our heavy life some rest;
Yet is not now the time so much o'erstay'd
   But that these words of mine which tow'rds thee move
     Must find thee still with spirit dispossess'd,
     And say to thee: "In Heaven she now is bless'd,
Even as the blessèd name[1] men call her by;"
       While thou dost ever cry,
"Alas! the blessing of mine eyes is flown!"
       Behold, these words set down
   Are needed still, for still thou sorrowest.
Then hearken; I would yield advisedly
Some comfort: Stay these sighs; give ear to me.

We know for certain that in this blind world
   Each man's subsistence is of grief and pain,
     Still trailed by fortune through all bitterness.
Blessèd the soul which, when its flesh is furl'd
   Within a shroud, rejoicing doth attain
     To Heaven itself, made free of earthly stress.
     Then wherefore sighs thy heart in abjectness,
Which for her triumph should exult aloud?
       For He the Lord our God
Hath called her, hearkening what her Angel said,
       To have Heaven perfected.
   Each saint for a new thing beholds her face,
And she the face of our Redemption sees,
Conversing with immortal substances.

[1] 'Beatrice' means 'she who confers blessing'. [Ed.]

Why now do pangs of torment clutch thy heart
  Which with thy love should make thee overjoy'd,
    As him whose intellect hath passed the skies?
Behold, the spirits of thy life depart
  Daily to Heaven with her, they so are buoy'd
    With their desire, and Love so bids them rise.
    O God! and thou, a man whom God made wise,
To nurse a charge of care, and love the same!
       I bid thee in His Name
From sin of sighing grief to hold thy breath,
      Nor let thy heart to death,
   Nor harbour death's resemblance in thine eyes.
God hath her with Himself eternally,
Yet she inhabits every hour with thee.

Be comforted, Love cries, be comforted!
  Devotion pleads, Peace, for the love of God!
   O yield thyself to prayers so full of grace;
And make thee naked now of this dull weed
  Which 'neath thy foot were better to be trod;
   For man through grief despairs and ends his days.
   How ever shouldst thou see the lovely face
If any desperate death should once be thine?
     From justice so condign
Withdraw thyself even now; that in the end
     Thy heart may not offend
   Against thy soul, which in the holy place,
In Heaven, still hopes to see her and to be
Within her arms. Let this hope comfort thee.

Look thou into the pleasure wherein dwells
  Thy lovely lady who is in Heaven crown'd,
   Who is herself thy hope in Heaven, the while
To make thy memory hallowed she avails;
  Being a soul within the deep Heaven bound,
    A face on thy heart painted, to beguile
   Thy heart of grief which else should turn it vile.
Even as she seemed a wonder here below,

On high she seemeth so, –
Yea, better known, is there more wondrous yet.
And even as she was met
First by the angels with sweet song and smile,
Thy spirit bears her back upon the wing,
Which often in those ways is journeying.

Of thee she entertains the blessed throngs,
And says to them: "While yet my body thrave
On earth, I gat much honour which he gave,
Commending me in his commended songs."
Also she asks alway of God our Lord
To give thee peace according to His word.

Anon (Old French)

John of Tours

John of Tours is back with peace,
But he comes home ill at ease.

"Good-morrow, mother." "Good-morrow, son;
Your wife has borne you a little one."

"Go now, mother, go before,
Make me a bed upon the floor;

"Very low your foot must fall,
That my wife hear not at all."

As it neared the midnight toll,
John of Tours gave up his soul.

"Tell me now, my mother my dear,
What's the crying that I hear?"

"Daughter, it 's the children wake
Crying with their teeth that ache."

"Tell me though, my mother my dear,
What 's the knocking that I hear?"

"Daughter, it 's the carpenter
Mending planks upon the stair."

"Tell me too, my mother my dear,
What 's the singing that I hear?"

"Daughter, it 's the priests in rows
Going round about our house."

"Tell me then, my mother my dear,
What's the dress that I should wear?"

"Daughter, any reds or blues,
But the black is most in use."

"Nay, but say, my mother my dear,
Why do you fall weeping here?"

"Oh! the truth must be said, –
It 's that John of Tours is dead."

"Mother, let the sexton know
That the grave must be for two;

"Aye, and still have room to spare,
For you must shut the baby there."

François Villon

The Ballad of Dead Ladies

Tell me now in what hidden way is
   Lady Flora the lovely Roman?
Where's Hipparchia, and where is Thais,
   Neither of them the fairer woman?
   Where is Echo, beheld of no man,
Only heard on river and mere, –
   She whose beauty was more than human?...
But where are the snows of yester-year?

Where's Héloise, the learned nun,
   For whose sake Abeillard, I ween,
Lost manhood and put priesthood on?
   (From Love he won such dule and teen!)
   And where, I pray you, is the Queen
Who willed that Buridan should steer
   Sewed in a sack's mouth down the Seine?...
But where are the snows of yester-year?

White Queen Blanche, like a queen of lilies,
　　With a voice like any mermaiden, –
Bertha Broadfoot, Beatrice, Alice,
　　And Ermengarde the lady of Maine, –
　　And that good Joan whom Englishmen
At Rouen doomed and burned her there, –
　　Mother of God, where are they then?...
But where are the snows of yester-year?

Nay, never ask this week, fair lord,
　　Where they are gone, nor yet this year,
Save with thus much for an overword, –
　　But where are the snows of yester-year?

To Death, of his Lady

Death, of thee do I make my moan,
　　Who hadst my lady away from me,
　　Nor wilt assuage thine enmity
Till with her life thou hast mine own;
For since that hour my strength has flown.
　　Lo! what wrong was her life to thee,
　　　　　　　　　　Death?

Two we were, and the heart was one;
　　Which now being dead, dead I must be,
　　Or seem alive as lifelessly
As in the choir the painted stone,
　　　　　　　　　　Death!

His Mother's Service to Our Lady

Lady of Heaven and Earth, and therewithal
　　Crowned Empress of the nether clefts of Hell, –
I, thy poor Christian, on thy name do call,

Commending me to thee, with thee to dwell,
    Albeit in nought I be commendable.
But all mine undeserving may not mar
Such mercies as thy sovereign mercies are;
    Without the which (as true words testify)
No soul can reach thy Heaven so fair and far.
    Even in this faith I choose to live and die.

Unto thy Son say thou that I am His,
    And to me graceless make Him gracious.
Sad Mary of Egypt lacked not of that bliss,
    Nor yet the sorrowful clerk Theophilus,
    Whose bitter sins were set aside even thus
Though to the Fiend his bounden service was.
Oh help me, lest in vain for me should pass
    (Sweet Virgin that shalt have no loss thereby!)
The blessed Host and sacring of the Mass.
    Even in this faith I choose to live and die.

A pitiful poor woman, shrunk and old,
    I am, and nothing learn'd in letter-lore.
Within my parish-cloister I behold
    A painted Heaven where harps and lutes adore,
    And eke an Hell whose damned folk seethe full sore:
One bringeth fear, the other joy to me.
That joy, great Goddess, make thou mine to be, –
    Thou of whom all must ask it even as I;
And that which faith desires, that let it see.
    For in this faith I choose to live and die.

O excellent Virgin Princess! thou didst bear
King Jesus, the most excellent comforter,
Who even of this our weakness craved a share,
    And for our sake stooped to us from on high,
Offering to death His young life sweet and fair.
Such as He is, Our Lord, I Him declare,
    And in this faith I choose to live and die.

Index of Titles and First Lines

Unto the blithe and lordly Fellowship   109

Was *that* the landmark? What, – the foolish well   34
Water, for anguish of the solstice; – nay   76
What is the sorriest thing that enters Hell?   39
What of her glass without her? The blank grey   32
What place so strange, – thou unrevealèd snow   38
What smouldering senses in death's sick delay   24
Whatever while the thought comes over me   127
When first that horse, within whose populous womb   40
When Lucy draws her mantle round her face   103
When the Troops were returning from Milan (Niccolò degli Albizzi)
    119
Whence came his feet into my field, and why?   42
Who is she coming, whom all gaze upon   133
Why did you melt your waxen man   80
Willowwood   30
Winged Hours   26
With other women I beheld my love   133
Within the gentle heart Love shelters him   104
Without Her   32
Woodspurge, The   92

Ye pilgrim-folk, advancing pensively   129
Yea, let me praise my lady whom I love   104
Young Fir-Wood, A   89
Your hands lie open in the long fresh grass   26
Youth's Spring-Tribute   25